STARTING-POINTS IN SOCIAL SCIENCE

BY

Albert Galloway

A. G. KELLER, Ph.D.

**PROFESSOR OF THE SCIENCE OF SOCIETY IN
YALE UNIVERSITY**

GINN AND COMPANY

BOSTON · NEW YORK · CHICAGO · LONDON
ATLANTA · DALLAS · COLUMBUS · SAN FRANCISCO

The Athenæum Press

GINN AND COMPANY · PRO-
PRIETORS · BOSTON · U.S.A.

PREFATORY NOTE

This collection of essays, dealing with elementary matters introductory to a study of the social sciences, was originally prepared and privately printed for intra-mural use in Yale University. Having been tried out for two years and having survived the ordeal, it is now given a wider publicity. The kind interest of the publishers enabled us from the first to present it to the student on the printed page, which was of great utility to the course involved. In the present edition the text and front matter have been relieved of certain features connecting the book with the local situation which it was originally designed to meet; beyond that almost no changes have been made.

The author has been much aided by the criticisms and suggestions of his colleagues in the course alluded to, and especially by those of Messrs. A. L. Bishop, R. H. Gabriel, and C. H. Ward.

A. G. KELLER

New Haven

CONTENTS

STARTING-POINTS IN SOCIAL SCIENCE

INTRODUCTORY: TYPES OF ENVIRONMENT AND OF MANKIND

The first starting-point for the study of things human is the natural environment of earth and air. Decisive for human life are the geographical factors of climate, topography, water-distribution, and the rest. For any region these determine also the type of organic life, and that life, in turn, forms an important part of mankind's environment. At the outset of this study the presence of the natural environment can be no more than suggested, and that may be briefly done by citing a few generalities and several typical illustrations, chiefly of types of organic environment and of the life lived in them.

In nature, death is always being transformed into life, and life into death. Chemical elements in the soil are taken up by plants and are transformed into vegetable matter. The plant grows and matures and presently dies; then its elements return to the soil what has been taken from it. Or the transformation may be more extended. The animal eats the plant, and the original chemicals are transformed into animal tissue. Man eats the animal, and thus appropriates the chemical substances in his turn. But, in the end, they are all returned to the inanimate world by the death of the man. He "returns to the dust."

In fact, animate beings die in part every day and hour; for they use up the cells of which their bodies are composed, and the burned-out cells are cast off in the form of dead matter.

There is, indeed, a constant flow of matter from the inorganic world into the organic, and then around back to the inorganic; from death to life, and from life to death. This is portrayed by Shakespeare in the well-known passage:

> Imperious Caesar, dead, and turned to clay,
> Might stop a hole to keep the wind away.
> O, that that earth which kept the world in awe
> Should patch a wall to expel the winter's flaw!

The next general fact to be noted is that the plant is an almost universal intermediary between animals and the inorganic world. There is very little in the way of nutriment that animals can take directly from the ground: water, of course, and salt are taken directly out of nature; but the chemicals that sustain life must generally pass through the plant before they can enter into the structure of the animal; so that while Earth is the mother of all things, the plant seems to be a sort of necessary channel through which the earth can nourish animal life.

It is a matter of common knowledge that plant life is dependent upon natural conditions, such as climate, rainfall, and soil, which occur in the inorganic world. In most treatises on physical geography attention is called to the kind of organic life that exists in various latitudes and altitudes, in deserts and well-watered valleys, and in the several kinds of soil. It would take volumes to list up the plant and animal resources of the various regions of the earth, and there would be no point in so doing; for our interest converges wholly upon man, so that we look upon plant and animal life, not as botanists or zoölogists, but in order to catch its bearing upon the life of man.

Hence, to illustrate the sorts of organic environment that man has encountered, we shall want only representative examples of the plant and animal life of several regions. These cases will be fair samples of a multitude of others where the combinations are different in various degree, but where the manner of working out the problem of living is along similar lines. Chiefly we are interested in what the less developed peoples have had to meet; but when we have got some idea of that, we shall naturally recall the plant and animal resources of civilized peoples. In the former case men have had to take what is presented to them; while in the latter, plants and animals not native to the country in question have been introduced into the environment and have become parts of it. As we call to mind the lowest and simplest cases of human relations to the plants and animals we shall see that, almost from the first, man begins to lay hand upon the plant and animal, controlling the destinies of both in his own interest.

The Bushmen of South Africa, who inhabit mainly the Kalahari Desert, the Australians of Central Australia, which is also extremely arid, and the Eskimo of Greenland, which might be called a frozen desert, are examples of peoples who meet a poor plant and animal environment.

The Kalahari Desert is one of the most barren parts of the earth, for there are no oases to speak of and the vegetation is of almost no utility to man. About the only vegetation accessible to the Bushman is a sort of melon which grows underground and which contains considerable water. It is useful mainly for the water it holds. The rest of the available food supply is game, such as the ostrich, and it too is hard to get, so that for a good part of the time the Bushmen go hungry. They eat any sort of animal matter that comes their way. As for protection (clothing and shelter), the other basic need of man alongside of food, they have almost none. A few sticks, propping up a shield of skins against sun and wind, constitute their building materials. Among their household effects are the shells of ostrich-eggs, which are also filled with water and buried in marked locations.

The Central Australians dig up certain roots and tubers, and annually feast to their limit upon the fruit of a certain bush, making long journeys, at the time of its maturity, to the spots where it grows. They hunt the kangaroo and other smaller animals, and have to keep on the move all the time, for they speedily exhaust the slight possibilities of any one region. A small group moves across the country in a long line, the women beating the ground with digging-sticks to detect the presence of the tubers and the men killing any kind of living thing which they stir up. They go over the ground, as it were with a fine-toothed comb, striving to keep life in their bodies by discovering every possible object of utility in the plant and animal environment. Clothing and shelter are slight, as in the case of the Bushmen.

The Greenland Eskimo inhabit a cold desert, and have practically no vegetable food, though they devour what they find in the stomachs of animals. They live chiefly on the seal and other sea-creatures, though they also kill bears and some other land-animals and hunt fowls. They are considerably better off than the Bushmen. Clothing is made of skins, and must be heavy and warm, and the summer tents are of hides, supported often with bones of large animals as a framework. Most of the Eskimo of this region have practically no wood except driftwood, being in a treeless country. A supply of good wood constitutes wealth.

These are extreme examples of peoples who inhabit deserts. Perhaps it is best to contrast their case at once with that of tribes which live amidst an abundance, or even a superabundance, of organic life. Certain of the Polynesians were so favored as to be able to lead an existence that was really too easy for their good. They had a profusion of vegetable food in the form of taro, breadfruit, tubers, and other products of tropical trees and plants. Fish swarmed in the waters about their islands and there were shellfish and turtles ready to be taken. The most important land-animal was the pig, which perhaps ought not to be counted in the natural environment, as it was doubtless brought to the islands. Birds of various sorts were at hand.

Altogether the life of these islanders was so easy that it caught the eye of the early voyagers, and some romancing philosophers, reading their reports, concluded that such a state of bliss must have been the lot of all men previous to the introduction of sin and its penalties. But any one who has caught any idea of the destitution of the Bushmen and other unfortunates realizes that there is nothing in this notion of the " golden age of primitive felicity "; and he who reflects on the matter, instead of dreaming about it, speedily notices that these islanders lacked the spur of necessity to urge them forward out of sloth; for they lived much as did the Lotus-Eaters of Homer and developed no important contributions to human culture.

It might be added that the Polynesians needed little clothing, and that what they had was ornamental rather than protective. They made a highly decorative bark-cloth, known as " tapa," by treating the inner bark, or bast, of one of their trees. Their houses were for protection against rain and sun rather than cold, and there was plenty of timber for frames and of reeds and leaves for thatching.

Ranged between the miserable environmental outfit of the desert-dwellers and the rich resources of some of the tropical peoples, have been the destinies of most of mankind; and they have approached the former rather than the latter. The arctic regions are almost always severe and difficult environments; but so, too, are many parts of the tropics. The very exuberance of their plant and animal life constitutes a peril and a handicap to men. In the Amazon region the vegetation is so dense that hardly any sunlight reaches the ground; plant life in the warm countries literally crowds man off the earth, and it is only with the most sustained effort that he keeps the jungle from overwhelming his fields and habitations. Let one recall the chapter in " The Jungle Book " which is called " Letting in the Jungle." Further, there exists in the environment a profusion of forms of animal and insect life that is highly unfavorable to man. Take the serpents; or the mosquito, which, in addition to the discomfort it causes, also carries the germ of yellow fever; or the *tsetse* fly, whose bite causes sleeping sickness.

The rest of our examples of environmental conditions encountered by backward peoples may be taken from the temperate zone. The Indians of the Great Plains of North America could hardly be anything else than hunters, for they inhabited prairie lands on which ranged great herds of bison and other smaller animals. There was fishing in the rivers, but that too is a form of hunting. There was wild vegetable food, such as the wild rice about the Great Lakes, and a very little cultivation provided what could not be got direct from nature. Clothing was made from deerskin; tents, or teepees, from coarser hides hung about a conical construction of poles. Life demanded vigor and exertion, but the materials were there.

Along the northwest coast the Indians were largely fishermen, for the supply available in the sea was large; and they developed skill in the making of dug-outs and other boats, and in the technique of fishing. In the East the tribes cleared the forests and developed, in addition to their hunting and mostly through the efforts of the women, a considerable agriculture.

When the horse was added to the Indians' environment by the Spaniards, the hunters quickly adopted it and became a mounted race, ranging over great distances in their hunting expeditions. The Indians were alarmed by the first horses they saw, and thought that the steeds and riders were composite beings; but later on the Indian himself came almost to be such, for he lived on a horse from boyhood up. When sheep were introduced, other Indian tribes adjusted themselves to their presence by becoming herders, living off their flocks and developing the process of weaving woolen rugs and blankets.

Other tribes over the earth, in whose environment were

animals capable of domestication, were led to become cattle-raisers. The Siberian tribes depend upon their reindeer; the South Africans upon their cattle. Their whole lives revolve about their flocks, and they talk and think in terms of their beasts. They wear leather clothing, in addition to subsisting upon the flesh and milk of their animals; and their shelters are either covered with hides or made of felted hair. They have fastened upon the one prime resource among their environmental conditions and are using it to its limit.

Our interest has been naturally shifting, as we have gone on, from the organic environment as a whole to special resources in that environment which have been singled out and made use of as the best expedients in living. Such expedients have been passed on from one people to another, and valuable plants and animals have been spread over the earth. Wheat was not native to America, but it is now part of its environment; similarly, maize has been carried from America to many other parts of the world. Any good book on commercial geography will reveal the extent to which such transfer of plant and animal resources has become possible.

Having suggested, thus sketchily, the permanent presence of inorganic and especially organic nature as a background before which all human rôles must be played, and having set certain undeveloped human societies against that background with the idea of illustrating, in lowest and simplest terms, the dependence of mankind upon the organic life existing in the natural environment, we now come to what must be an almost equally casual glance at the several varieties of mankind. Several types of environment, as encountered by man, have been indicated. Against them man has been set in such manner as almost to suggest that he is a constant quantity. He is not that. All men are essentially alike—so much so, at least, that they have generally been classified all together in one species. Nevertheless there are human differences which, even though relatively superficial, are yet capable of resulting in quite diverse social destinies. Since our interest centers upon the social life of mankind, we must take account of factors which so weightily influence its character.

THE RACES OF MANKIND

Man, it must always be borne in mind, is a late-comer upon the earth. Evidence is lacking that nature stood reverent, submissive, and expectant of his arrival. For untold ages the world got on without him, the tides rose and ebbed, the rocks were eroded, vegetation sprang up and withered away, the beasts were born, grew to maturity, and died. Into this natural environment man was, at length, introduced. The forms of life which were already here did not give way before him and let him have what he wanted and needed; he had to come into the struggle as best he could. No seat was reserved for him at the "banquet of life"; if he got a place he had to push some other form of life out of it. He was not wanted. He had to force his way in.

He succeeded in doing this, and most of what follows in this essay is an account of the way in which he learned to help himself. But before we come to that, it is necessary to survey the various types of mankind which came into contact with the environment as sketched above. Such types are called races. The term "race" is usually applied to any large body of human beings having characteristics in common which set them off from other human groups.

Classifying human beings is like classifying any other mass of objects which, when seen as a whole, is bewildering in its confusion; it is a matter of patiently noting the likenesses and unlikenesses which exist among them. Correspondence is classified by distinguishing letters as coming from different persons, treating of different topics, or otherwise. Then all the letters which are found to have the same origin or subject matter are filed together. They are separated on the basis of their differences, and united on that of their similari-

ties. No two letters are totally unlike, nor yet exactly alike;
to classify them, certain characteristics are selected which lie
somewhere between their unlikenesses and their likenesses.

Similarly with the classification of mankind: if you go into
the most minute, microscopic peculiarities, no human beings.
not even twins, are exactly alike; to classify them exactly,
each would need to have a separate pigeonhole. On the other
hand, if only the broadest characteristics, such as general
bodily structure, are considered, then all men are so much
alike that they would all go into the same pigeonhole. In
either case, classification is defeated. Somewhere between the
minute characteristics, which are too small to be useful in
distinguishing types of mankind, and the general ones, which
are too comprehensive, lies a set of likenesses and differences
upon which a workable classification can be made. This is
the sort of classification which we seek.

It is evident that any classification of mankind will be
simple or complicated according to the generality or particu-
larity of the points upon which it is based. Human beings
have been divided, on broad lines, into as few as three races —
the Black, White, and Yellow — and, on narrower lines, into
upward of sixty races. The fewer the classes, the rougher the
classification. Our classification, which is a rough one, but all
we need for our purposes, will recognize five main races: the
Negro, the Mongolian, the Malay, the American Indian, and
the Caucasian.

In no classification of living beings — for organisms shade
into one another, up and down the scale, by almost imperceptible degrees — can one hope to draw hard and fast lines,
and to include every individual safely, entirely, and forever
within a single division. In the case of the correspondence,
part of a certain letter may belong to one file and part to
another, or it may fall between two files. So in the case of a
human being, or even of a group of them: members of a
certain tribe may show the Mongolian type in most respects,

and yet have a shape of head that is not Mongolian. There may also be a sort of half-way type between two races, which would have a division to itself if any more divisions were allowed. You have to stop making divisions somewhere, or you get down in the end to as many classes as there are men, and then you are at precisely the place where you started. One has always to be warning himself, when he is sorting out living beings, that he is doing an artificial thing; for nature is full of shadings from form to form that refuse to be herded into man-made classes. It is necessary to classify, or we should be lost without bearings in the multitude of forms; but we should never get the idea that our divisions are all-inclusive, inevitable, and eternal.

One more word before we come to the actual classification. It is not to be understood that the races were created as they now are. Both science and Scripture assert that all mankind came from one stem or stock; and if this is so, all must have been originally pretty much alike. Further, all must have come from some one part of the world. We do not try here to take up the story of mankind from the beginning, but are, for the moment, seeking simply to give an idea of the varieties of mankind as they are encountered today.

Physical differences are the ones with which we naturally begin. The most obvious basis upon which human races are classified is color of skin; and the five races just mentioned may be called the Black, Yellow, Brown, Red, and White. This is an old and familiar classification; it corresponds well enough to the facts, and there is nothing to be gained by introducing a new one. Further, a number of the other physical characteristics go with color; thus, the Blacks generally have long heads and flat noses; and so color might be considered a basic characteristic. This five-fold classification turns out, also, to correspond with geographical location: the Negroes are native to Africa and Australasia, the Mongolians to eastern Asia, the Malays to the Malay Archipelago and adjacent regions, the Indians to America, the Caucasians to Europe and western Asia. All races have wandered more or less; but we are now speaking of their original locations, so far as history reveals them.

Aside from color of skin and geographical location, these five races are distinguished by many other characteristics, mental and cultural, as well as physical. Holding to the physical, we find them differing in color of hair and eyes; in stature; in size and weight of brain; in shape of head, nose, and lips; in texture, length, and shape (cross-section) of hair; and in the presence or absence of the beard in males. These are perhaps the surest marks of race, physically considered; in any case, they will serve our purpose. The five races show these characteristics as follows.

African Negroes are, in general, dark of skin, eyes, and hair; tall of stature; comparatively small and light of brain; long of head; broad and flat of nose; with lips thick and everted; hair short, coarse, and woolly; beard slight or absent. The Australian type of Black rather exaggerates the African; but the lips are thinner, the hair long and wavy, and the beard heavy.

Geographically, the Negro is divided into two main groups: the Eastern Blacks and the Western. The former occupy Australia, Tasmania, New Guinea, and the Melanesian Islands; the latter, Africa south of the Sahara, and including the western half of Madagascar. There are tribes in southern India that are generally classed as Blacks, and several scattered peoples, called Negritos (Little Blacks), in the Philippines and other islands to the southeast of Asia.

The Mongolian race is yellowish of skin, and dark of eyes and hair. The so-called oblique eye is sometimes called the " Mongolian eye." This race is short of stature; medium as respects size and weight of brain; broad-headed and flat of face; with a small and low nose; thin lips; coarse, long, and straight hair; and little or no beard.

This race occupies most of the northern and eastern parts of Asia, including Siberia, Mongolia, Manchuria, China, Japan, Korea, Indo-China, Tibet, and Chinese Turkestan. The farther from Mongolia and Manchuria, the more the Mongolian type merges into surrounding types. In the west the Lapps, Finns, Magyars, and Cossacks show Mongolian relations. The Eskimo, who reach from the northeastern tip of Asia across North America to the east coast of Greenland, are classed as Mongolian.

The Brown (Malay) and Red (American Indian) races are much closer in physique to the Mongolian type than to the White or Black. It is probable that the Malay is a mixture in which the Mongolian element is strong, and it is generally accepted that the American Indians once emigrated from Asia. In the case of these two races, we need cite only their main divergences from the Mongolian.

The Malays are of a golden or light-brown skin, and the eye often does not show the characteristics of the "Mongolian eye." They occupy the islands southeast of Asia as far as New Guinea, and extend northward through the Philippines and Formosa to Japan. A western branch inhabits the eastern half of Madagascar.

The so-called Red race, or "Redskins," as they were called by the "Palefaces," are really copper-colored of skin. They differ from the Mongolian type in stature also, for they are tall; in head-form, which is medium rather than broad; in shape of nose, which is higher than the Mongolian; and the eye is not "slanting." They occupy America except for the fringe of Eskimo along the Arctic coast.

The Caucasian, or White, race has generally a light skin, dark to light hair and eyes; medium stature; large and heavy brain; head medium between long and broad; face often narrow; nose often thin and high; lips medium between thin and full; hair fine, medium in length, and generally wavy; beard

present and often heavy. Two types of Whites are distinguished: the Dark Whites and the Light.

The Light Whites are native to northern Europe; the Dark
Whites, to the rest of Europe, northern Africa, southwestern
Asia, and northern India. The following peoples outside of
Europe are generally classed as Dark Whites: Persians, Ar-
menians, Hebrews, Arabs, Egyptians, northern Hindus, and
the Berbers of southern Algeria, Morocco, and Tunis.

The above classification takes account of all considerable
peoples except the Polynesians. These are similar in a number
of respects to the Malays, though some of them might be
taken for southern Europeans. They differ from the Malays in
being brown of skin, tall of stature, and in having curly hair.

If such physical differences were all that could be discovered, they would amount to little or nothing in a study of
the development of human institutions. A straight nose does
not, of itself, make a good trader, nor does woolly hair prevent
a race from developing a high civilization. Except for the
fact that physical characteristics accompany certain types of
civilization, they might, for our purposes, as well be omitted.
It is only when we realize that, for instance, no woolly-haired
people has ever attained a high civilization, that we come to
suspect some connection between physical characteristics and
mental capacities; for we associate mental ability with the
attainment of civilization. We must next look into this matter
of mental characteristics and into the degree of civilization
reached by the several races.

Mental differences must be of dominant significance; but
they are not so obvious or so easily measurable as might be
thought. To say that one race differs from another because
its members have better minds is an easy way to dodge a
complicated question. What is a " better mind "? Is it one
that was brought into the world better and of higher quality?
Or is it one that has been improved by experience and train-

ing? Some intellects are so constitutionally feeble that no amount of cultivation can make anything out of them (as well try to turn a cabbage into a rose by careful gardening), while others may well have been cultivated so thoroughly that they look and act like good instruments, though they might not have been so promising to begin with. It is next to impossible to say just what percentage of mental power is natural endowment and what part is acquired cultivation. An inferior mind, well cultivated and disciplined, may be a better one for all practical purposes than a superior mental machine that has been neglected and allowed to rust.

There is such a thing as sheer mental power, which belongs to a man by reason of his heredity; but still a great deal depends upon what is *in* that mind. What a brain can do depends not only upon what sort of instrument it is, in its original make-up, but also upon what it has stored up within it, to work upon. For our purpose it does not matter very much whether minds are better because of original endowment or because of cultivation. We are interested more in what people's minds can *do*, as indicated by the results they have got, than in any analysis of what lies behind mental action, even though that could be accurately made.

No person of judgment would want to assert that the Australian Black has as good a brain as the European. It is not important that his brain is lighter and smaller—his nervous system in general less sensitive and adjustable. It is in all ways probable that, with the best of cultivation, from birth on, his mind could not be raised to the European level. But in most racial comparisons it is not possible to be as sure as this. The question is always rising to plague one as to whether an apparent superiority is not due to what is in the mind rather than to the quality of the mind itself.

The so-called lower races (meaning generally the Black, Brown, and Red) usually develop as much mental power as they need under their circumstances. Because a savage cannot count above ten, there is no reason for denying him a mind. He does not have to count higher than that to get along well enough in life. His ancestors have not had to, and so there is no store of knowledge along this line for him to learn. No one who has actually studied savage life ever harbors the impression that the native is a fool. His mind is often very keen when applied to familiar problems that confront him daily in living. As his life is not complicated, his mental processes do not have to be. He is a close observer of nature: for instance, he excels the white man in his ability to follow a trail; he can judge accurately the time that has elapsed since a certain foot-print was made; he can extract information from such evidence with a skill that leaves the civilized man mystified. Judging savage intelligence by its success in solving the life-problems that challenge it, considerable mental ability must be accorded to many individuals and groups of individuals among the " lower races."

It takes a combination of favorable conditions, both natural and social, to bring out mental capacities and possibilities. A person born with the best of mental endowment could not make much of a showing if from babyhood he had lived in solitude on some unvisited island. Whether there is much or little in the mind, whether it is cultivated or not, depends upon its surroundings. The white man's superiority is often not so much in native intelligence as in the fact that he has at disposal an accumulation of experience and knowledge gathered by preceding generations, and stored in tradition and written record, an accumulation unknown to savages. The white man may not have an abler mind; but he knows more. Even the dull school boy knows more about a number of things than Aristotle, one of the most powerful minds of all time; he uses algebra, for example, about which the Greeks knew nothing, for it had not yet come into being. What appears to be mental superiority is often only that which is taken up out of a richer environment of things and men.

Thus the distinction between mental endowment and mental outfit or content is a real one, even though in many cases it is exceedingly difficult to draw. The White and Yellow races seem to have the better minds; they have also developed by far the greatest part of the civilization and knowledge possessed by mankind. They appear to be less emotional and impulsive, less childlike, than the other races. That such qualities, whatever their origin, are an advantage in the struggle of races is proved by the predominance of the peoples who possess them.

We can, it is now clear, distinguish the races of men pretty well on the basis of physique, although that distinction means little for our present purpose, which is the study of institutions, such as property, law, and government. We can distinguish them only vaguely and uncertainly on the basis of mental powers, if by that we mean original, innate endowment of mind. But if we take as a basis of distinction the degree of civilization attained by the use of mental powers, we find the matter of classification clearing up. We have something definite to go on. Popular usage has already applied the adjectives " savage," " barbarous," " half-civilized," " civilized," to grades of difference along these lines; races are called " lower " or " higher " according as they show an undeveloped or a developed civilization.

A civilized race is also called a cultured race. We shall wish to use this word " culture " to cover all those evidences of civilization which men have developed through the ages. Culture may be material or immaterial: thus a stone ax is a piece of culture, just as is a gas-engine; buildings, roads, docks, vehicles, boats, air-craft — all these are items that go under material culture. The habit of keeping the peace, instead of quarreling all the time and fighting it out, is an evidence of culture; so is a market, a credit-system, traffic-rules, game-laws, and all other arrangements by which men get on together better. These latter arrangements are immaterial; that is, you cannot go and lay a hand on them, or measure or weigh them, as you can with material things. Still more immaterial, perhaps, are literature, art, and music; the word culture is often reserved to cover these finer and least material of man's acquisitions. But we wish to use it more broadly.

Everyone knows what the terms " savage," " barbarous," " civilized," mean. Classification on the basis of culture is a natural one, based upon distinctions general enough to be recognized by all. For our purposes it is worth more than any of the rest; but it also falls in with the others to a considerable degree. In general, the Black race has always remained on a low grade of culture; and that attained by the Malay and American Indians has been, on the average, very moderate. Portions of the Yellow race (in China) had reached a relatively very high degree of culture while the rest of the world was still, for the most part, in savagery. But they have been overtaken and passed by the White race, which has shown the highest civilization in history. The white man's culture has spread over the earth, and has exercised a varied influence upon the other races, ranging from extermination and degradation to stimulation and improvement. Only the most civilized sections of the Yellow race have been able to rally their forces and assimilate the civilization of the White race, so as to appear as its rivals, potentially if not actually, in world-domination.

It is this civilization or culture, as developed by the several races, which is to be the prime object of our study. We shall now, in the main, give our attention to the culture rather than to the races. But all that we shall find out about it will throw back light upon our classification of the races of men.

HUMAN ADJUSTMENTS

CHAPTER I

THE FACT OF ADJUSTMENT

We have now seen something of the influence upon man of the natural environment in which he lives, and of his actions amidst the conditions to which his life is exposed. The study of trade, one should note, is a sort of key-study; for the development of trade forms a sort of sample, or epitome, of the development of civilization in general. Before we undertake to discover the nature and mode of development of that civilization or culture by which, as we have seen, the races of men are characterized in differing degree, we must make a preliminary study of a great law that operates in the lives of all living beings; and we shall have to go back to the plant and animal world to get a start. This law can be led up to by a set of examples.

It is prohibited in some cities to plant poplar trees along the streets; and it takes only a slight acquaintance with the tree to see that such an ordinance is not a foolish piece of meddling with personal liberty. The poplar will send out rootlets in all directions in search of more nutriment, and if they encounter a sewer or water-pipe, they will seek out the smallest crack in it, or in the cemented joints, and will force their way in. Once inside, the rootlet will grow rapidly into a dense mesh of branches, and presently the pipe will be stopped up and there will be no flow of water, or the sewer will back up into the house. This performance has caused the poplar to become unpopular. Looked at, however, from a scientific standpoint, the tree is seen to be wonderfully well fitted or adapted for the securing of what it needs in order to live and flourish.

The plant world is full of instances even more striking than this. There is a certain orchid which needs, in order to propagate, what is called cross-fertilization, which means that pollen must be carried from one plant to another. It is accomplished in the following manner, and quite involuntarily, by bees. Above a cup in the orchid, which is full of water up to a spout-like opening, there is a deposit of sweet material which the bees eagerly gather. They push one another about while so doing, and presently one of them falls into the cup. The only exit for the wet-winged victim is by way of the spout, which is a tight fit for her. While emerging, the bee is obliged to rub first against a sticky substance and then against a deposit of pollen, which adheres for a time to her body, but at length drops off upon another orchid visited by the bee. Thus is cross-fertilization secured. It is evident that the plant is well adapted to secure what it needs in order that orchids shall continue to grow.

The animal world shows adjustments quite as effective as these. The works of the great French observer, Fabre, on wasps, spiders, glow-worms, and other insects, teem with almost incredible instances.

Let us take a pair of cases from among the larger animals. The polar bear, living in arctic regions, has a coat which is thick and which sheds water, and under it a layer of non-conducting fat which retains his bodily heat. Further, he is white in color, which makes him difficult to see against the snowy background — like a black cat in a dark room. In the case of weaker animals this " protective coloration " enables them to evade their enemies. The polar bear has no enemies that he fears, except man, and so his coat is hardly protective; but it allows him to steal up on his prey, the seal, until he is able to make a short dash and catch it before it can dive into its hole in the ice. The seal sleeps for brief intervals between short periods of scanning the landscape; and the bear has the added advantage of an instinct which causes him to remain motionless, or " freeze," during the seal's reconnaissance. The bear's body and instinct are well adjusted to food-getting, and so to the prolongation of his life.

The camel is another clear case. An ancient story among desert-dwellers represents the horse as being dissatisfied with his physical make-up because it was not suited to travel in the desert. He teases the gods for this and that alteration — a longer neck, padded feet, power to endure thirst, and so on — until they lose patience with his complaints and bring out a camel, which has all the qualities he was asking for. The story says that the horse trembled at the sight, and that all his descendants have always shivered in the presence of the camel. The latter, having the power of closing his nostrils in a sand-storm, of going for long periods without water, and of skimming over soft and shifting sand on his broad, cushion-like feet — not sinking in, but as if on snowshoes — is well provided with bodily adjustments to the sort of country he frequents.

Men too show such physical adjustments. Color of skin seems to be one of them; for the Negro will expose his body without ill effect to the tropical sun, while the white man is speedily and severely burned, and runs the danger of sunstroke. Again, the Negro of the west coast of Africa, while he sometimes gets fever, is likely to suffer little where the whites die off like flies. It is evident that the native of any country is likely to be better adapted physically for life in that environment than is the immigrant, especially if the native's ancestors have lived there for generations. There are many regions, especially in the tropics, where the white man literally cannot exist if he tries to live as the natives do, without any protection or remedies against climate and disease.

Here is a set of physical adjustments occurring in plant, animal, and man, which are often so perfect that no uninstructed person could conceive of how they came about. They were therefore referred to an omnipotent, supernatural power, that is, to the gods. No one could blame the savages for that, for these adjustments were evidently too fine and remarkable to be the work of human hands, and the idea of the workings of natural law was still a thing of the remote future. It was not, indeed, till the middle of the last century that the natural process, under natural law, which secures such apt adjustments, was discovered and demonstrated by Charles Darwin. His evolutionary theory is vulgarly identified with the phrase: " Man is descended from a monkey "; as a matter of truth, it is concerned primarily with the explanation, under natural law, of the adjustments of plants and animals to their life-conditions. The evolutionary theory is, in essence, a theory of *adjustment*, or *adaptation*.

Before we follow the Darwinian explanation of how adjustments come about, it is necessary first to consider another class of adjustments. It should be noted that these words, adaptation and adjustment, are used all the time in common talk. Such and such a device, say an electric trolley, is said to be well adapted to modern conditions; while a stage-coach, well adapted to Washington's time, would be anything but an adjustment today. The fact of adaptation and maladaptation, adjustment and maladjustment, has always been seen and acknowledged, both in the world of nature and in the realm of social life; the only difficulty has lain in accounting for that fact.

The new class of adjustments which we must note are those which men make, as they cannot make orchid-cups or horses' hoofs; they are the electric cars, stage-coaches, and other devices which constitute both material and immaterial culture. Their nature may come out best by considering first some very simple cases of adjustment along this line.

The savage wants to climb a tall palm. He encloses his

body and the trunk of the tree within a ring of rope, somewhat like the strap used by the telephone lineman, leans back against the rope, and walks up the tree, hitching the rope up the trunk as he goes. Without the rope he was but poorly adapted to such climbing. The rope-ring is his adjustment, just as a cat's claws are hers. Similarly, the lineman puts on his climbing-irons, and is then at least partially bear-like in climbing ability. If man ever invents something like a monkey's prehensile tail, he will be the better adjusted to getting about among the branches.

Again, an American is about to visit a country where the sanitation is notoriously bad. He fears the typhoid germ. But he resorts to the process of inoculation against this disease, and is thenceforward much better adapted to live and thrive amidst the new life-conditions.

A traveler in South Africa is taking an incautious stroll, unarmed, out on the veldt, and notices a tawny animal crouching in the grass and manifesting a disquieting interest in him. He is for the moment rather poorly adapted to go on living in that region. But his servant suddenly rushes up and thrusts into his hands a double-barreled express rifle, loaded with explosive bullets. Now he is adjusted pretty well, especially if he has made himself a good marksman, to an erstwhile dubious situation. Formerly he had only his teeth and nails to oppose to the lion's fangs and claws, at close quarters; now he can hit the beast a deadly blow long before it can come within striking distance. His range is much increased; and if the rifle were a cannon, he could lengthen that range by many miles.

Examples of non-material adjustments to life-conditions are as numerous as the material. A tribe of savages who have no chief and no laws making for discipline, but who are always quarreling and fighting among themselves, are periodically set upon by their neighbors, and a number of them killed and wounded. They try to take vengeance from time to time, but do not succeed, for the neighboring tribe has a chief who maintains discipline, posts sentries, and drills his warriors. For life under savage conditions the former tribe is poorly adapted by reason of the lack of that organization, the possession of which renders the latter tribe well adapted, as proved by the outcome when the two come into collision.

Two communities exist side by side. In the one, everybody makes all his own clothing, tools, and other implements and belongings; in the other, division of labor and specialization are in vogue. In view of the advantages and economies which, as anyone can readily see, inhere in these arts and practices, the second group prospers over the first, lives where the first starves, lives better where the first merely exists, grows wealthy where the first remains poor. For by its system of specialization, through which, as anyone observes, time, effort, and material are saved, and yet a better product attained, it is better adapted to its life-conditions. After a while it will probably wipe out, enslave, or buy up its rival.

Take one more case from savage life. It is imaginary, in the sense that no tribe without the adjustment to be mentioned has ever been discovered; yet that adjustment is not in nature, and so there must have been peoples, at some remote time, who did not possess it. Suppose two tribes side by side, one of which has no belief in spirits and gods, and the other of which fervently believes in them and in the effectiveness of magic. The two tribes come into collision. The first fights for life as well as it can, with whatever weapons and organization it has; but the second has an extra resource. It goes into battle with magical preparation, and such preparation is far from futile. The gods have been sacrificed to, the omens have been taken by inspection of the entrails of chickens and found to be favorable, and the medicine-man has anointed the warriors and their weapons with some magical substance which, he assures them (and they believe it serenely and unshakenly), will both prevent them from being killed and will make their spears deadly to the enemy. Other things being anywhere nearly equal, the fanatical confidence of the second tribe will bring victory. The tribesmen with the winning spirit and enthusiasm are better adjusted to their life-conditions than the people who have no such confidence. Napoleon ranked spirit, or "morale," as by far the most important factor in war. Thus religious beliefs constitute an adjustment comparable to the fierce temper of the hornet. Consider the wild valor of the Moslems, which is rooted in their religion.

All examples of adjustment do not by any means come out of savage life; but they are easier to observe in their simpler terms. Our own life is full of such adaptations. As New York City grew, the very necessities for living in such numbers and in such proximity had to be provided. No great city could exist for a week without a system of waterworks and sewers. Without them, though they were not needed when the Dutch first settled there, Manhattan Island would speedily be swept by disease. They are adjustments allowing of existence under the life-conditions of crowding. Nor could such a mass of people feed themselves; the milk-supply of New York City is forwarded daily from distant points. But that calls for a system of regular and rapid transportation; the railroads, as well as the sewers, are an adjustment to life-conditions. Every day, we are told, about four thousand additional fares have to be carried by the transportation system of the city itself; and the result is the necessity of almost daily adjustment to the heavier demands, unless discomfort, loss of time and money, and even deaths by accident are to be allowed to increase. Meanwhile the traffic on the streets grows daily heavier, and necessitates revision and re-revision of traffic-rules, which represent adjustment as truly as does the rifle of the hunter; for without them life could not be lived, or, in any case, could not be lived fully, but only in a crippled and painful manner.

Modern laws are just as much adjustments as are the edicts of the savage chief. Lawlessness is a synonym for general misery, and usually means death for somebody, or a number of bodies. If people are going to live together, they must adhere to rules of conduct; and these rules are developed to meet life-conditions. The law is a shield by which a man can protect himself in a manner in no essential differing from the use of a buckler by a warrior, or of a shell by a turtle. Law is not a material thing, but it does the job if it is in a healthy condition and has developed to serve what it is designed to protect, not leaving portions of its protégé's anatomy open to assault.

All these adjustments are themselves in process of evolution whereby they change form as circumstances change. Government is not an adjustment established once and for all, nor is religion. If any adjustment does not alter to suit change in conditions, it becomes a maladjustment. It would never do to transfer a Zulu chief to the White House; he would be a misfit; and so would an American President in Fiji. Democratic government, where the people are to rule, was never developed at all during the vastly greater part of man's sojourn on earth, and it would be wholly maladapted to many backward peoples of the present day. The religion that suited the Pilgrims and Puritans cannot meet the conditions of today; much less can the type of belief and practice that constituted the religious adjustment of the warlike ancient Hebrews. In fact, the religion of the city is different from that of the country; to the rustic the city usually seems godless. Perhaps the doing of no work for one-seventh of the time is possible on isolated farms; but such a suspension in a big city would be in utter disaccord with life-conditions, and would certainly involve wide discomfort, and even sickness and death.

The enforcement of a law prohibiting Sunday labor would evidently be, not an adjustment, but a maladjustment. To have prohibited " jay-walking " at country cross-roads two centuries ago would have been foolishly unsuitable. Thus it appears that what may constitute an adjustment at one place and time, under the local life-conditions, may be no adjustment at all at another place and time. Out-of-date adjustments become nuisances because they have turned into maladjustments.

We have now reviewed a set of cases of physical adjustments in plants and animals, and have seen that mankind too exhibit some physical adaptations, which constitute the physical differences between the several races. But men do the bulk of their adjusting by developing material instruments, which do for them what is done for animals by claws and other bodily parts, and by working out methods, systems, and various other immaterial arrangements for dealing with the problem of living in various environments and in various contacts with fellow-men. It remains to say, with respect to these social arrangements, that they too have been commonly ascribed to supernatural power because their origin could not be otherwise accounted for. It is generally a god who is said first to have generated fire or invented the alphabet; it is a godlike or inspired law-giver, like Minos or Moses, who " gave " the laws. So that here too, though the fact of adjustment is perceived, there has been much dispute as to how it came about.

If the idea of adjustment has been sufficiently illustrated, it has become evident that it is a great fact of life. It exists on all sides, and a very child could cite numbers of cases when once his attention had been called to the idea. It was certainly a notable intellectual feat, however, to discover how adjustment of life to life-conditions came about in the organic world, and to suggest the presence of a parallel process working within the social life of mankind.

But before we go forward to examine into the theory of adaptation, it remains to make the connection between the fact of adjustment and that thing we call civilization, or culture, which is possessed in differing degrees by the various peoples of the earth. The connection is simple, though not self-evident. These adjustments, in the shape of tools, weapons, transportation, laws, government, religion, and the rest, *are* civilization or culture. What else could civilization be except these? In popular usage these are, perhaps, the evidences or accoutrements of civilization, the word civilization itself being reserved, it may be, for the state of mind of people who have developed all these aids in living. But it is common enough in describing the stage of civilization of any people to make a list of such adjustments, material and immaterial, as we have reviewed, and to expatiate upon their life-preserving and comfort-affording function. It was customary even in Homer's time to describe savagery or uncivilization, as in the case of the Cyclopes, by recounting the absence of such adjustments as the civilized and cultured have.

No reasonable person could object to the statement that the *ways* in which people meet their life-conditions afford a measure of their culture. And it is an astonishing fact, when one first confronts it, that peoples tend to meet similar life-conditions in remarkably similar ways; to make similar adjustments. This occurs under conditions where it is virtually certain that they could not have borrowed from one another. Trivial adjustments to situations that are not at all vital, as in styles, show the widest variety; but when it comes to exigencies that are universal to the human race, and of great significance, such as the need of internal peace and co-operation in the face of danger, the adjustments developed are much the same for all peoples whose lives have not come to be too complicated. Thus savage government, with small exception, is of pretty much the same type; and so are primitive property-systems, forms of marriage, and religions.

As social life becomes more complicated, there are more divergences, and the various institutions of one civilized people come to differ from those of another, as is not the case among the backward tribes. In any given nation the various institutions take on a sort of national type, for they all have

to be consistent with each other if the life of the society is to
go on smoothly. The transportation system of Siberia would
not fit in with the business organization of America; even our
railroads are having difficulty in keeping pace with demands.
The religion of China could not harmonize — ancestor-wor-
ship, conservatism, and all — with the institutions of England,
though it has been concordant with the rest of the Chinese
institutions for many centuries. Thus nations develop institutions with a sort of family resemblance between them, and of
a type differing in many respects from those of other nations.
But the essence of the big and important institutional adjustments remains the same for all nations, for the basic needs that
summoned them into being never disappear, and mankind has
settled down, all over the world, into almost a single way of
meeting them. It is always necessary for any society to combat
lawlessness and disorder, and all societies have had to develop government and law. Such laws always forbid such
actions as have been found to incite to strife, namely, murder,
theft, and other wrongs; and they assure life, property, and
other " rights." The commandment against killing and steal-
ing stands, as an adjustment, as strong today as it did in the
time of Moses. These big, vital adjustments are necessary to
society's life in all ages, and it is by their persistence and
strength that society lives on.

Sets of adjustments, finally, are likely to develop around
some large interest of life, attending to its various details, and
forming a sort of jacket for it. One of the big interests of life
is satisfying hunger and protecting the body from injury by
cold and heat; and around this interest have gathered many
sets of adjustments which we call agriculture, manufacture,
commerce, and so on, and can include under the term " industrial organization." Another big interest is the relation of men
to the supernatural, and the set of adjustments attending to
that relation we call religion. A third major interest of mankind — in fact, one of the prime life-conditions — has to do

with the matter of sex. The race is divided into two sexes, very different one from the other, which must live along together. As a consequence, there are all sorts of ways of securing adjustments between them. Sometimes, for instance, there is one man to several wives; again, several men to one wife (polyandry); and yet again, one man to one wife. Then there are provisions about who may not marry whom, or about the property that must pass as bride-price or dowry, or about the children and their rights. All these, and the form of the family as well, are adjustments whereby life may be lived at all, or lived more easily. All of them taken together are called marriage, the marriage *institution*. Likewise there is an institution of religion and of property.

We have met the term "institution" before; it has been used without comment hitherto. Now we must try to get a more definite idea of what we are to mean by the term, in this course on the development of human institutions. Institutions are blocks of adjustments centering about some important human interest. In seeking to trace the development of human adjustments we are therefore searching for the key to the development or evolution of social institutions. "An institution," says Sumner ("Folkways," § 61), "consists of a concept (idea, notion, doctrine, interest) and a structure." The structure is the framework or apparatus, and may be only a number of functionaries set to coöperate in prescribed ways under certain circumstances. "The structure holds the concept and furnishes instrumentalities for bringing it into the world of facts and action in a way to serve the interests of men in society."

And now we must drop institutions for the time, to return to them when we have followed up the process discovered by Darwin by which the adjustments of plants and animals come about.

CHAPTER II

THE MODE OF ADJUSTMENT

The adjustments of plants and animals are not in their own control at all; they are brought about by forces on the outside, to whose action the adjusting organisms are subjected. Plants and animals do not feel the need of adaptation and then somehow devise and put into operation the necessary structures. The cat does not have claws because he wants them. If one animal is better adjusted than another, it is his fortune, not his merit. Adjustment is brought about by the action of impersonal, automatically acting factors. In the plant and animal world these are three in number, and might be called *unlikeness, competition,* and *likeness.* Darwin named them *variation, selection,* and *heredity.* Though we cannot, in the present instance, follow the action of these factors except in the most general way, yet in order to understand adjustment we must get a broad perspective of their nature and their work.

The factor of *unlikeness,* or *variation,* brings it about that no two plants or animals are duplicates of each other as, for instance, newly minted coins are duplicates. This unlikeness hardly needs to be dwelt upon much, for everyone, upon reflection, admits it. No two kittens of the same litter are exactly alike. Two seeds of the same plant may seem to be precisely alike, but upon microscopic examination they are seen not to be so. Sometimes the differences are large, again very small, but they are there. In one investigation, the muscles of the human foot were found not to be strictly alike in any two out of fifty bodies. It should be clear enough, without further illustration, that plants and animals show endless differences.

Such differences, representing inequalities of endowment for living, might not be revealed if there were no contest or *competition*. It takes a foot-race to prove who has the best equipment for running; you can tell something from inspection, but the actual test is the only reliable basis of judgment. And all plants and animals are under test all the time, for they have to engage in an unending struggle to live. There is seldom food enough for all; there is a continuous competition for what there is; the weaker have to struggle also not to become the food of the stronger.

To comprehend the nature of this competition—the intensity of the struggle for existence—it is necessary to realize that any plant or animal form, if let alone, would speedily populate the whole earth. This means that all that are born shall live to maturity and breed. Reproduction is a rapid geometrical progression, and one should reflect upon the incredible speed with which a geometrical progression piles up. If, for instance, a man be given one cent the first day, two the next, four the next, and so on, for thirty days, he would receive as the thirtieth gift $5,368,709.12. But this is an increase of only double the amount per day. Take, now, the case of an animal producing ten pairs each year to each pair, and each animal living ten years. There would be eleven pairs alive at the end of the first year, one hundred and twenty-one at the end of the second, and so on until, at the end of the twentieth year, the number of pairs would be represented by the number seven with twenty ciphers after it. In the case of oysters, which breed much more rapidly even than this, the great-great-grandchildren of the first pair would reach the number sixty-six followed by thirty-three ciphers. Estimated as oyster shells, these results of a few years' reproduction would have, it is calculated, a mass several times the size of the world. These are staggering figures and sound, prior to verification, like fever-ravings.

It is plain that we have no such number of oysters, even

after centuries of reproduction. Where are the missing billions of billions? Evidently they never grew up. There must have been a tremendous death-rate, due chiefly to the fact that the young fell a prey to devouring enemies. Where there is no such check to keep numbers down, the increase promptly appears. In Europe rabbits have their competitors and enemies, but when they were taken to Australia, where there were no animals to prey upon them, they speedily overran a large part of the continent.

All plants and animals struggle for life, and will not be crowded out of it without resistance. Hence the struggle for existence. And this struggle is so severe, and so many are engaged in it, that even a small favorable difference may mean life, and a slight inferiority death. It is the plant or animal with the inferior equipment that must die; and that leaves the better equipped to survive. The elimination of the less fit, whereby the field is left to the more fit, is called *natural selection*, or *the survival of the fittest*. To cite one case, the fish that can leap the farthest out of water when pursued by an enemy, staying in the air the longest and entering the water again at a distant point, is the one that lives on, while those that can "fly" for a shorter distance are caught and eaten. Under the existing life-conditions the former is better adjusted than the latter. Thus the more effective adjustment is preserved.

Those that live on are the ones that produce the young which are to be the next generation; and now comes in the fact that offspring are like their parents. Here is the factor of *likeness* or *heredity*, which preserves the winning qualities and carries them on to succeeding generations. Thus will a whole race of beings—not occasional individuals only—come to have advantages in the struggle, such as thick hide, dense fur, powerful wings, gripping talons, keen scent, and all the rest of the wonderful adjustments seen in nature, cases of which have been cited. No one has taken thought to produce these, but the natural forces have worked them out automatically, just as they have brought it about that objects fall toward the center of the earth by gravitation. Given the factors of unlikeness, competition, and likeness — or variation, selection, and heredity — and the result must be *adjustment to environment,* or *to life-conditions.* Because there is unlikeness, there is an advantage of some over others in the struggle for existence; and because there is likeness between the survivors and their offspring, the qualities of the successful are fixed and perpetuated, so long as life-conditions do not change.

If they do change, then the fittest are no longer fittest, and new variations — for variation is always taking place — have their chance. Thus adjustment may pass into maladjustment. The appearance of the brown-tail moth and the gypsy moth in New England meant a change in life-conditions for vegetation, and certain of the formerly flourishing shade and orchard trees came to be maladjusted, and have suffered greatly. The white man, without intending to do so, imported the tuberculosis germ into the Pacific islands, and the natives have perished of consumption in large numbers. They were unfitter than the whites in their resistance to the germ. The latter have suffered considerably from the disease, and so are not fully adjusted; but the Polynesians showed almost total maladjustment. Such maladjustment is readily explained by the evolution theory; but any theory which holds that all beings were fashioned to be in happy adjustment, has its difficulties in accounting for unhappy maladjustment.

Charles Darwin provided a key for the unlocking of nature's secrets in the matter of adjustment in the organic world; and he at least uncovered a clue for the explanation of that adjustment which human beings living in society practise through the agency of inventions, methods, systems, and institutions, as illustrated in the preceding chapter. There can be no understanding of the full force of the evolution theory without thorough study of Darwin's works and those of his successors; but the central fact of adjustment as a law of life, and the operation of the factors that bring it about, can be apprehended by anyone who will give his attention to it.

It is clear that animals and plants must adjust themselves to their life-conditions or decline and die out. So must human beings. If people in a cold climate refused to wear clothes, or to live in houses, or to heat the houses they live in, in winter, a heavy death-rate might be expected. There must be adjustment, not only to the change of seasons but to the change of weather. Food and fuel must be accumulated against the cold period; when coal is not mined and transported to meet the needs of different regions, suffering and even death result. No race can afford to bid defiance to its life-conditions, whether they are natural or social. Preparedness in the face of a war-like and treaty-breaking neighbor is an adjustment that a nation neglects at its peril; the result may be annihilation or, what is worse for a proud people, enslavement. Even if the subjugated people do not die, their nation and their civilization are likely to perish.

But human beings do not adjust in precisely the manner of animals and plants, by physical changes whereby, for instance, fins, fur, keenness of scent, and the like, are developed. They "use their heads" to do their adjusting, and not their bodies. Human adjustment is *mental* rather than physical, and the adaptations by which men live are products of the mind rather than bodily modifications. This does not mean that they are deliberately devised and thought out in all or even in many cases, any more than plant and animal adjustments are. It is only that the brain is especially sensitive to external conditions, and takes on the adjusting function for the body. No one, for instance, ever thought out beforehand and then worked out in practice the system of division of labor; it worked itself out of the experience of life, little by little, as people fumbled about, tried this and that expedient, noted what sort of action paid best, and repeated it, while discarding less successful procedures. The fact is that the brain is the great organ for variation, that is, for producing new ideas. It keeps throwing them out into the stream of social life, where they sink or swim, according as they prove to be expedient or inexpedient. The patent-office is a museum of ideas embodied in inventions — variations, some of which have amounted to nothing, whereas others, surviving the competitive test, have made living far easier and more satisfactory for great numbers of human beings.

It is essential to realize, before we try to trace the development of these mental adjustments into institutions, that none of man's important adjustments ever sprang into being complete and adequate, like the fully armed goddess from the head of Jove. All of them have had a long past of growth and improvement out of extremely simple beginnings. When one of them, say a system of laws, is referred to some god or mythical law-giver, as his exploit, this means only that the adjustment is so old that its origin is unknown; for it has ever been the custom of mankind to refer the unknown to the supernatural. And if such an adjustment is credited to some man, it generally means that he furnished the last and often small item which made the adjustment effective, as in the case of an invention. Consider this latter case for a moment.

It is said that a certain man, named Howe, invented the sewing-machine. But we know that plenty of men had been working toward it for some time, and that it was Howe who came along to put on the last touch and get his name attached to the invention. And then, back of Howe and all his rivals, lay the efforts of others who found out how to temper steel, work iron, and otherwise provide the materials without which Howe would have been helpless. Back in the elder ages women had learned to make bone-needles and sinew-thread; and behind them all stands the inventor of the process of fire, without which metal-working could not have been, nor, indeed, could men have lived, except in the warm parts of the earth.

Every inventor stands on the shoulders of thousands of men long dead, and every invention goes back to very simple adjustments, some of them hardly recognizable as the forerunners of the present forms.

If we seek for the beginnings of human mental adjustments, we get some such picture as the following. In those earlier ages men were faced by needs, as they always have been; but the early ones were simple and vital, calling for food and for protection against cold, wild animals, human enemies, and other perils of all sorts. If adjustment to such life-conditions were not somehow managed, life could not go on at all, or with any approach to safety and comfort. Necessity was the mother of invention. It must be understood, however, that early man had no stores of experience to go by, and no idea of the relation of means to ends. He knew he was cold, or hungry, or imperilled, or otherwise uncomfortable, and he began to wriggle and squirm to get out of his trouble. He reacted like a child, in an undirected, rather hit-or-miss manner, upon the situation. These reactions were mental *variations,* even though they were not planned and thought out.

In the presence of need, it might be said that early man tried everything. When hungry, for instance, he ate anything he could lay hand on, including earth, insects, and human flesh. But some of his variations in meeting his needs succeeded better than others. If they were altogether inexpedient — for instance, if he chanced on poisonous food — he perished. If certain of the variations were better, those who practised them lived on and kept up their practice. If some members of a tribe hit upon ways that were superior to all others, as proved by their success in avoiding pain and winning satisfaction, the rest presently imitated those ways of meeting needs, dropping others, and the ways became customs in the tribe. Such customs were passed on by tradition to the next generation, or even over to a neighboring tribe. Here, in the very origin of customs, appear the factors of *unlikeness,* or *variation* — in the differing reactions of different individuals; of *selection* between reactions — where the unsuccessful ones are given up; and of *likeness* — in the *transmission*, by imitation, of successful reactions. The adjustment-process is already in swing, however crude and simple the ways of meeting arising needs may be.

For our purposes, however, we may take up the story at the point where the trial-and-failure or trial-and-success process, in the face of needs, has resulted in customs practised by groups; so that each small group of human beings has a set of stock ways for meeting types of situations. To get food, for instance, the method of a certain people is always hunting, with bow and arrows; to keep warm, there have been developed cloaks made of skin; for shelter, there are huts, always conical in shape, made of sticks and mud; as a defense-organization, there is a chief and some drill in fighting; to combat disease, there is sacrifice to the ghosts of the departed, together with fasting and blood-letting. No one thinks of doing differently, when the need appears, but all act in approximately the same way.

It is at this point that the actions in the face of need become *mass-phenomena;* that is, they are characteristic not of individuals alone, but of whole groups of people, or human societies. It is here that they enter the field of our study, for until they are mass-phenomena they cannot develop into the institutions of society. They do not become customs till they are practised in concert by a number of people; and it is out of customs that all institutions develop.

Its customs are, indeed, the most characteristic things about a group of human beings. They constitute its civilization; and we have seen that even the largest groups, the human races, are most commonly distinguished on the basis of their degree of civilization or culture. Any stage of civilization is characterized by its customary ways of living, that is, by its peculiar sets of mental adjustments to life-conditions. These may be material things, such as tools and weapons; processes, such as hunting or agriculture; systems, such as division of labor or slavery; organizations, such as the family or state; sets of beliefs, such as magic or religion. A people that shows no agriculture, a polygamous family organization, an unlimited despotism, and a belief in witchcraft is readily distinguishable from one whose members, as a whole, understand tillage, practise monogamy, live under a constitutional monarchy, and profess to believe that God is one. Upon such contrasting sets of adjustments to life-conditions, peoples can be distinguished from one another at least as readily as upon the basis of physical differences.

Here is the element of unlikeness, or *variation* in customs. All human groups, however small, down to and including the family, have their own peculiar customary actions or conduct in the face of life-conditions. No two families, even on the same street, have the same ways — treat their children, for instance, in the same manner; for the presence of children certainly constitutes an important life-condition. No two classes in the same society, no two religious bodies, no two towns, or states, or nations have identical customs. The differences may be greater or less, but they are there. This factor of unlikeness, or variation, between the customs of human groups, needs only to have attention called to it; for it is observable all about us.

But this unlikeness means that different groups enter *competition* with different chances of success. All human groups are striving to live and to get ahead in the world; and to do so, they must compete with one another. The group possessing the best adjustment to its natural environment is likely to win, other things being equal; and the same is true of the group with the best organization for handling both friendly and unfriendly contacts with its neighbors. Their elements of superiority or inferiority lie in their adjustments — in their weapons, wealth, discipline, organization — far more than in mere physique. The competition may be warlike or peaceful. If it is the former, then all these things count very obviously. If it is peaceful — in industry, trade, or politics — still do the more expedient methods, organization, and instrumentalities prevail. Consider to what a degree, under the stress of competition, the organization of modern business has been developed; in order to survive, it has been necessary to keep up with all the new adjustments in accounting, marketing, and advertising, just as in war it has been necessary to have the best accoutrements and drill, the most modern inventions in the way of battle-ships, submarines, and mines. It is the severity of competition that brings out the new variations in response to pressing need; thus the air-craft underwent a forced development during the war-years 1914–1918, which a decade of peaceful competition might not have brought about.

This is about the same as saying that competition, here as elsewhere, issues in *selection*. A fight, whether bloody or not, is a test, where some win and others lose. Sets of customs are selected for decline or extermination, while others survive as constituting better adjustment. In the competition of groups those who win power carry their customs to victory with them, for it is by the fact of winning that the customs are justified, at least in the eyes of the conquerors. Those who are overcome are sometimes obliged to give up some of their peculiar customs, as the South had to renounce slavery — which amounted to the selection of slavery for extinction, together with the survival of a fitter system of freedom. In this case of the Civil War, what happened was something as follows. There grew up in America, in the eighteenth and the first half of the nineteenth centuries, owing to the presence of differing environmental influences, climatic and other, two divergent types of culture. That of the North was based on free labor, and it developed democracy; that of the South on slave labor, and it developed aristocracy. The customs and views of the two sections were so diverse that an irritation arose between them, so intense as to make it impossible for them, as they were, to live together peaceably within the same nation. They came into conflict, the South fighting for liberty and freedom to do as it pleased, like the original Thirteen Colonies, the North to prevent the South from destroying the nation. The result was not simply the destruction of slavery, but the destruction of the whole Southern type of civilization. The economic collapse of the South that resulted from the war and the Reconstruction Period, contributed, along with the freeing of the slaves, to this result. Thereafter ensued a period wherein the South has been taking on the ways and institutions of the North.

The masses of people do not think these big aspects of things out, least of all beforehand; something brings on a conflict, on the battle-field or at the polls, and a general shake-up takes place, out of which emerges a victory for sets of ideas and customs that were not seen by many, beforehand, to be part of the issue at all. Out of the Civil War, for instance, came the development of a high protective tariff; the tariff of 1857 was low, and people seemed contented with it; then duties were raised as a war measure and have never sunk to the pre-war level again.

The substitution, through selection, of new customs for old takes time; but there has been plenty of that, if of nothing else, in human history; and if time is given, the result is sure. Adjustment and readjustment will take place forever; for life-conditions change, and customs must change to meet them. But there are some broad adjustments to life-conditions that are permanent, so far as we can see, if society is to endure. There must always be law and order within a society, and so there must always be discipline and government. Anarchy will not do. Where a certain long-tested set of ways, for instance a property-system or a religion, has persisted under ages of competition, it must constitute, however unreasonable it looks from certain angles, an essential and efficient adjustment in living. This should be considered by radicals who want to upset property, the family, or religion in favor of certain bright ideas or dreams which have occurred to them in their discontent with things as they are. It is doubtful whether improvement in adjustment has ever been won by destruction of what is, with the idea of starting all over again on some " logical " system. The successful readjustment is attained generally, if not always, by small alterations rather than by turning the world upside down. Revolutions are not the sudden happenings which some people take them to be.

So much, for the present, about the factor of *competition,* with *selection,* in social adjustments.

There remains the factor of likeness, though it cannot, in its connection with adjustment through custom, be called heredity. We shall speak of it as *transmission.* All these ways and customs are transmitted or passed on to the next generation, or even across to a neighboring group. They are sometimes called " the social heritage," a term which indicates a popular and proper appreciation of the likeness between the transmission of customs and the inheritance of physical and mental qualities; but it is a term which is misleading. For these adjustment-ways are never inherited, as physical qualities are, but are *learned.* Language is one of the adjustments developed long ago in response to the social need of communication; yet no baby is ever born able to use or by himself to develop the control of this important instrumentality. Each generation has to learn it anew. Color of skin and stature are inherited; control over the adjustive instrumentalities of society is acquired mainly through imitation of those who are familiar with them.

In any case there is here a factor which, like heredity, secures descent of tested variations, keeping them the while close to the traditional types, preserving the expedients that have survived under competition. So that the customs of a society are not alone spread, chiefly by imitation, among all who are living together at a period, but they are kept to the same type through time. Like heredity, transmission (or tradition) is a conservative factor, and is likely to suppress new variations. It is a sort of balance-wheel in society. If we had variation only, we should have a chaos of new and perhaps wild ideas; if we had tradition alone, we should be in the midst of the changelessness and immobility of death. But when we have the outreachings of variation controlled and balanced by the steadying factor of tradition, we get a happy medium, which allows of a continuous readjustment that does not unduly " rock the boat."

It is the new and " raw " countries that have no traditions; and their life is often portrayed as a helter-skelter affair. They are ready to try anything, but are without any background of experience to make them critical. They have " wildcat " banks, let us say, or " frontier-justice." Impostures of all sorts flourish, from the charlatan at the county fair to the lightning-rod agent. Such countries are generally colonies on the frontier of civilization. It is true that the colonists have a set of traditions which they have learned at home; but they have had to forget or ignore most of them under the new life-conditions. There is something to be said for such new societies as the originators of new ideas, for their variation is exuberant and is not restrained by tradition; but they have to settle down somewhat before they are really respectable members of the concourse of civilization. We shall see more of this type of society later on.

An extreme of the traditional type is an old nation which has resided long in the same place, and has become stiffened and unable readily to adapt. This stiffening is due to the suppression of variation by tradition; for variation is the prime necessity, if there is to be any adaptive change. Such a country is China. Centuries ago the Chinese were the most civilized people of the earth; but they got into a rut and came to feel that what was good enough for their ancestors was good enough for them; and they clung to tradition all the more closely because their religion was the worship of their ancestors and the carrying out of what was supposed to be the ancestral will, that is, traditional usage in all the affairs of life. Thus the balance-wheel of tradition turned into a brake on progress. For ages Chinese culture was too strong to yield before the competition it met; but when it encountered the civilization of the West, its weaknesses were speedily revealed.

If one wants further illustration of the absence and presence of tradition, let him compare some new university with Harvard and Yale or with Oxford and Cambridge.

The most successful adjustment in living is attained through a balance of the two elements — a fact which is attested by the tendency of the new society to acquire traditions, and by the falling behind of an old society which is tradition-ridden. Neither extreme type attains successful adjustment.

We see, then, that the same factors produce adjustment, whether it be in the plant and animal world or in the life of human societies. The law of all life is adjustment, and everywhere in life it is attained in the same general way. It is possible to go much more deeply into the process than we have done; but for the present purpose we do not need to scrutinize all the details involved. We return now to a consideration of the *sum of adjustments* of various human societies, that is, to their *civilization,* in order to note the development of these adjustments into *types of civilization.* Institutions, we noted, at the end of the chapter on The Fact of Adjustment, are blocks of adjustments. We have stopped to consider the process of adaptation before going on with the development of the institutions.

CHAPTER III

THE FOOD–QUEST

If we seek to learn how man has built up those sets of mental and social adjustments which go to make up civilization, we must go back for our start to the life of the uncivilized. For in their adjustments we have a sort of base-line from which to take our departure. The lower down we can begin, the better, for it gives us a longer sweep of development. Also we shall see the adjustments to life-conditions, which are now so complicated and difficult to understand, in their lowest terms; for the ways of savages generally reveal simple and easily understandable reactions in the face of needs common to all men.

So far as direct evidence goes, we know of no peoples who have been utterly destitute of tools, weapons, and other such non-bodily adjustments to life-conditions. But, since the animals have none of these aids in the struggle for existence, it is necessary to believe that man was once without them. There are some tribes on earth who have almost nothing to help them except fire, a few poor implements, the scantiest of clothing, wretched huts, the loosest form of organization in labor, the family, and government, a defective language, and the vaguest type of religion. If we could subtract but a little from what they have, they would be naked animals, inferior to the rest of brute creation because they would lack the physical adjustments — strength, speed, scent, and the like — which the beasts possess. No people is in all respects at the lowest known stage; but such tribes as the aborigines of Australia, the Pygmies and Bushmen of Africa, and Veddahs of Ceylon, or the Fuegians of Tierra del Fuego, give us a pretty good clue as to what human destitution must have been in the period when men had nothing but their bare bodies with which to fight the battle of life.

It is possible to picture the life they led, under such circumstances, by imagining one of the lowest tribes we know bereft of what little civilization it has. The only way to live would be by wandering about picking up what food could be found and seized upon. This would include vegetable matter which could be plucked, pulled up, or easily dug, and such animals as could not fight or escape. The most backward tribes eat a variety of poor and, to us, repulsive food that is easy to get. The shores of several continents reveal great heaps of shells left by untold generations of eaters of shell-fish, which were about the only sort of non-vegetable prey that existed in profusion and could not resist or get away. Even in this case, however, the eaters must have had a weapon, though it scarcely deserves the name, in the shape of a stone or stick caught up and used to attack the shells. Even such a poor instrument opened up an important food-supply.

In most cases, where men had no instruments of any kind, they could not have lived close together, for the country, as they were able to utilize it, could not support them except in small bands which must always be on the move, working out an area and then moving on. They could no more than skim the surface of the food-resources of a region. Population was sparse and generally underfed on poor food. Periods of starvation were recurrent and the death-rate high. The people were always skirting along the ragged edge of the abyss, and it took only a small jog of ill luck to push them over. They had little defense against their enemies of the animal world, and, in addition to searching for food, had to keep from becoming themselves food for their enemies. A reconstruction of life under such circumstances appears in Jack London's story "Before Adam."

If we could find a people destitute of all aids in the struggle for existence, we might take it as a zero-line from which to start in tracing the course of civilization. But we cannot go behind the actual cases, as described by travelers, of certain observed and still existing human tribes. In making a series it really does not matter whether you start from zero — nothing — or a little farther up the scale; if ninety be taken to represent modern civilization, that figure is not much farther from the zero of peoples with no real civilization than from the one, two, or five of the lowest known tribes.

One can get at the basis of society's life most quickly if he confines his attention at first to the mere food-quest, noting the development of adjustments to the conditions of its prosecution. In so doing, he will be dealing with the most basic and essential of all activities, for if that quest is unsuccessful, the stage is presently cleared of all actors, and the play is done.

The lowest tribes that have been observed are in possession of implements which can generally be used, in the pursuit of a livelihood, as either tools or weapons. A great many of them can be readily traced to one or the other of two originals, or to a combination of the two, namely, the stick and the stone. Descendants of the former are most cutting and thrusting implements, such as the club, spear, arrow, sword, knife, awl, needle, saw, and auger; while from the latter are derived all missile-weapons. From a combination of the two come the ax, mace, hammer, adze, and, in general, all instruments with a head and handle. Consider first the rough club and the unwrought stone. They are used as they happen to present themselves, but each is so formed by nature that it is preferable to any chance stick or stone which one might catch up on the spur of the moment.

That such a stick or stone in the hand is an adjustment has been sufficiently explained in foregoing pages. The stick is more efficient in digging for roots than the bare hand can be, and with it a heavier blow can be struck, at longer range, than with the fist or foot. Armed with a stout club, man is equalized with animals which he could not overcome before. With the stone he can strike a blow at arm's length, bringing down the grasped rock, which is as good as a hand of flint; or he can hurl it as a missile, thereby greatly increasing his range in striking. He can, by learning to throw accurately, completely neutralize the superiority in quickness possessed by some animal hitherto easily able to escape him. Without following this case into detail, we may readily see that a man thus armed is greatly strengthened in the battle of life as compared with his unarmed state.

The bow-and-arrow is a typical implement of the chase. What we have here is a little spear, which, through the utilization of the springiness of the bow, is thrown with great velocity and penetrating power. Gradually, under the instruction of experience, through a series of variations, accidental at least in part, the arrow receives a stone or bone point, perhaps with barbs, and is feathered to steady its flight. In some countries all the other qualities of the arrow are subordinated to its efficiency as a carrier of deadly poison; it needs only to scratch the skin of the victim, not to penetrate deeply. Then the bow comes to be made out of the most elastic wood, or horn. Through a long course of improvement there are developed at length the yew bow and goose-feathered shaft of the English bowman. The acquisition of skill in the use of the weapon is another part of the combined items of adjustment.

Equipped with a bow such as the Indian knew how to make, a sheaf of arrows, and skill in manipulation, the hunter for game or fish — for fish are frequently shot with arrows — is several times the food-getter he was before. It may seem to us that the bow is a device much inferior to the shot-gun, but that conviction, like many another that seems obvious, is not wholly true. The bow, like the blow-gun, operates in virtual silence, and does not scare off the game. For the savage's purpose it is a better adjustment than the fire-arm, and some savages have discarded the latter to go back to it. Of course, when the fire-arm is equipped with a silencer, its special point of maladjustment is removed. In any case the man plus the bow-and-arrow is much fitter for the struggle for existence than the man alone. It is necessary to note that he has taken things out of nature, and adapted them to his uses; and in particular that he has appropriated energy out of nature— in this case the elasticity of wood, bone, or horn. Much of man's adjustment, as we shall see later, has lain in the capture and control of natural forms of energy, such as the mechanical energy of gravity or torsion, or the chemical energy of fire, gun-powder, or even food itself. Falling water and the heat and light of fire are specific examples.

Hunting-equipment includes, besides weapons, also traps, nets, fish-hooks, skin-floats, canoes, and a myriad of other expedients. A tribe possessing a share of all these no longer needs to live so much from hand to mouth, or to remain so helplessly subject to the chances of life. Its adjustment is much bettered. It does not so lightly skim the food possibilities of land or water. Population can be denser and is better fed and conditioned. The death-rate is lowered There are even intervals of leisure for the satisfaction of more than animal needs. Nothing succeeds like success, and the better adjustment breeds confidence. The hunting tribe is on the way to further adjustments; but, as the figures of population on the hunting stage show, it is not yet able to support many persons per square mile. And one should not overlook the fact that weapons may be used for defense as well as for offense, not alone against the animals but also against fellow-men. The armed tribe can keep the food it has from being taken away; it can defend its food-preserve, or hunting-ground; and its members can resist being made food of by man-eaters, whether animal or human.

Other weapons and devices for the food-quest might be cited, and their evolution traced — from the blow-gun to the rifle, from the dug-out to the steam-trawler — but the story is always the same: successive small improvements, suggested by accident or incident, raise the originally rough and clumsy adjustment to the complicated and elaborate one. The ingenuity of the savage hunter is often very great, but he stands at the beginning of a long line of improvers, and cannot reach the results attainable by a much inferior ingenuity standing on the shoulders of generations of predecessors. It is wonderful that the Eskimo can work bone as he does. When it is all he has, he makes it go. But of course his bone spear-points are not as effective as steel ones, and his spear is not in the same class as the whaler's harpoon-gun. His skin canoe is, like the Indian birch-bark craft, a marvel of lightness, and unrivaled in its adjustment to certain conditions; but it is no rival, for general purposes, to the motor-dory. Each such item in the hunter's equipment has an evolution of its own over ages of variation, selection, and transmission.

Among the adjustments in the food-quest one of the most important ever made by man is the domestication of animals. The antecedent set of adjustments here needed are those of the hunting stage, for they include methods and devices for catching animals alive and unhurt. It is probable enough that the hunting type of culture almost invariably preceded the type characterized by the possession of domesticated animals, and that the latter evolved by variation from the former. However that may be, the process of domestication may be taken to have started in something the following fashion.

Since animals represented to man primarily a food-supply, and must be killed in order to serve that purpose, it is clear that there must have been a superfluity of food available before animals were kept alive instead of being slaughtered. Men early developed the art of drying and smoking meat, to preserve it against the future. Suppose, now, that a tribe had enough food for its present and prospective needs, and yet had caught some young animals alive. There was no reason to kill them except joy in destruction. In any case the fact is that such superfluous animals were kept and tamed. The dog was one of the first, if not the first, to be spared and attached, alive, to man's destiny. The first idea might well have been to preserve the meat in living form, to be available at need. But once the animals were spared and attached to man's life, a variation had been set afloat which led presently to a new set of adjustments.

For when man had animals about him, under conditions where he had a deep practical interest in them and observed their qualities more closely, he naturally killed off the less desirable, in time of need, and saved the best; then the best bred together, and after a time he possessed something better in quality than the beasts as he took them out of nature. This is what has been called " unconscious artificial selection," or accidental breeding. Man early came to notice not alone the variations in animals, by which some pleased him more, some less, but also the fact that offspring resembled parents; and when he had at length caught the possibility of taking advantage of these conditions, he took upon himself the function of selection; that is, he saw to it that what he considered to be the type fittest to his needs should survive. After a while he deliberately bred his domestic animals and produced " breeds " that possessed qualities superior, for his purposes, to those of the wild animals. Thus man, at first unconsciously, and later deliberately, adjusted his actions to the laws of nature and succeeded thereby in adapting his whole life more satisfactorily to life-conditions.

Some of the details of artificial selection and breeding have doubtless come within the experience of most readers; we see man get his results by taking the differences, small and great, presented to him by animal variation, and adding them up through the utilization of heredity. This is a pretty high-grade operation in adjustment, taking more mental alertness than the rude shaping of stone. It has been seen that savages seldom possess a good breed of animals; and that is because their general level of culture is too low. They have no adequate enclosures, so that they cannot keep their animals from mixing with inferior or wild strains and thus " losing the breed." They cannot hold by heredity the favorable variations that are offered to them.

The start in domestication and breeding once made, new possibilities of adjustment meet man from time to time, and he has presently appropriated, not the animals' flesh alone, but many of their powers, such as strength and speed, besides. It must always be kept in mind, however, that all this development came, in the first instance, from the food-quest; for there are few animals (or plants) which were not first domesticated and bred for the sake of food. The dog and horse, the flax and hemp, were of interest at the outset, and still are in some regions, not at all, or not alone, for service in hunting or transportation or for the use of fibers in making fabrics, but for their value as food. If we are seeking the ultimate basis of any of these human adjustments, we are generally safe in searching for its utility in preserving life.

When men have once climbed to the possession of domesticated animals, especially of the larger ones, like cattle, their food-supply is steadier and better. They are much better adjusted to life-conditions than they were before. They have to move about a good deal, with their flocks and herds, from pasturage to pasturage; but they can live together in larger numbers, which always means that they have a better chance to develop further civilization. The death-rate is lower and the general level of comfort is higher. There is more leisure from the stark struggle for existence. In fact, with every new and more adequate set of adjustments, men get farther away from that struggle, until they are competing rather for comfort and luxury than for the bare necessities of life.

In pursuing the evolution of the food-quest we come now to the domestication of plants. With few exceptions food is either animal or vegetable. Strictly speaking, it might be taken to include water and salt; and water is present in all vegetable and animal substances. Salt is a greater exception, being a mineral; but it enters into the plant and animal substance, and is strongly craved by man. Aside from such partial exceptions, food, we say, is either animal or vegetable matter. Some animals are carnivorous, eating little or no vegetable food; while others are graminivorous, rejecting flesh. Man is omnivorous, as some of our examples indicate; in some regions he eats earth, though it is for the organic matter in it rather than for the earth itself.

The domestication of plants would seem to be easier than that of animals. It is not. It takes more patience and foresight to save and plant the seed and cultivate the crop than to preserve captured animals. For the captive animal can be killed and eaten tomorrow or next week, while the seed, once entrusted to the ground, is spoiled as food and, to get a return, one must wait for a considerable time. The patience and foresight demanded for such operations are just the qualities developed under civilization and which the savage has not. Also the plant must be protected, and worked over, and relieved from the competition of undesirable rivals (weeds), while the herds are at first half wild, like the reindeer, and are more like game in a preserve than domestic products.

The mere collection of roots and grains which were growing in a wild state was perhaps the earliest form of the food-quest, and the earliest agriculture is but little removed from it. Many peoples gather, at the time of ripening, to harvest natural crops like the wild rice of the Great Lakes. Some have taken the next and significant step of planting; yet they do not cultivate much or at all, but simply plan to be present, on the spot, when the plants have matured and can be harvested. It is seen here, once again, by what gradual steps man attains to a successful adjustment, learning the ways of nature a bit at a time, and conforming to them; accumulating small experiences and fitting them together until he arrives at what might be called a real invention.

To get very far in the art of agriculture, it is necessary to possess domestic animals, for until great power, like that of the ox or horse, is available, men cannot plow very extensively and deeply. Without that power, what is done might better be called horticulture, or gardening; it is sometimes called hoe-culture. The development of agriculture is conditioned also by the previous development of tools and implements, chief among them fire, for land-clearing—which is an exceedingly arduous matter, especially where vegetation is dense and quick-growing. Once started, though, the development of new methods and knowledge goes on apace; the possibility of restoring to the land those chemicals known as plant-foods, by the use of ashes, manure, fish, and the rest of the fertilizers, is discovered by noting their effects when accidentally applied the soil. Rotation of crops is another adjustment of the first importance. It is to be noted that the early farmers never knew why these processes had such effects; they merely noted and remembered that they did promote fertility. Thus, by trying this and that and retaining or discarding, according to the results attained, men developed agriculture from the crudest forms to a high productivity.

By plant-breeding men got results similar to those attained in animal-breeding—increase in quantity and quality. Plants which were at first raised for food were at length found to be useful as producers of fibers, and interest shifted from the seeds to the stalks. It is almost unnecessary to say that all the effects upon population and general well-being, mentioned above in connection with hunting and herding, here appear in a higher degree. Not only, however, could an area of land support more people, in greater comfort, under agriculture, but its population became sedentary. They did not wander, not being able to take their crops with them as they could take animals, but stuck to their gardens and farms. In general, wandering about is not conducive to the development of civilization, while " staying put " is. A rolling stone gathers about as much moss as a roving people does of culture. Few hunters or herders have developed much civilization; the very earliest cultured peoples were tillers of the soil, in Egypt, Mesopotamia, and the river regions of India and China.

The process of adjustment in food-getting might be followed into minute and multitudinous detail. There are many devices in hunting, many different kinds of domesticated animals and plants, each worth investigation for its evidence as to the pushing and prying nature of man's efforts, under the spur of necessity, first to keep alive and then to attain satisfactions over and above the mere minimum of existence. However, there are really but two general methods of food-getting: hunting for it as it exists in nature, or raising it; and there are but two ways of raising it, namely, by herding and breeding, or by tillage. But, whether in hunting, herding, or tillage, the essence of the activity is finding how things go in nature, and then adjusting to natural law so as to make use of all the advantages that may accrue for human life and welfare. Every adjustment made by man in laying hand to food, whether in the form of a bow-and-arrow or a domesticated animal or plant, gave him a better chance to live or to live well; for in every case his food-quest was lightened and he was removed ever farther from the very edge of existence, where some slight calamity might at any time push him over.

CHAPTER IV

THE TRANSFORMATION OF MATERIALS

Next to food, men need protection from the elements; and such protection, in the form of garments or a house, must be made of materials drawn out of nature, and shaped to the uses of man. Even food is usually somewhat transformed before it is eaten; and when it comes to other materials, like clay or metal ores, they are of no utility until man has " made " them, that is, transformed them into something different as to shape or other qualities.

In strict truth man has never " made " anything of a material order since he appeared on earth. There is not an extra ounce of matter in the world for whose presence he is responsible. He himself is of dust and to dust returns. The sum-total of matter remains the same — unless one should wish to count the meteoric additions — as it was when man had not yet arrived on the planet. What he has done is to re-form matter into other shapes, as when he carves a stone; transform one thing into another, as when he burns coal; combine this and that, as when he " makes " bronze out of copper and tin; take things apart, as when he evaporates sea-water to get the salt; put things in the way or take them out of the way of forces, as when he dams or clears a stream; divide forces, as when he splits an electric current (which he has " made " by putting such things together as will generate a current) and sends it over several wires. In short, man gets his effects by manipulating things existing in nature.

To do this, he needs to know the properties and nature of the materials and forces which he attempts to use. He can change the qualities or the laws in no respect, any more than he can create the material or force originally. All sorts of ill success, disappointment, self-injury, and violent death appear as penalties for interference with the natural course of things. Man cannot push his way through nature at will, in the absence of special knowledge. It is the last which enables him to adjust his action to the actual conditions that surround him. This knowledge started at zero and has been painfully acquired by trial and failure over thousands of years, the results having been committed to tradition and passed on to succeeding generations. In this chapter we are to review some of the earlier and simpler re-shapings and transformations of natural materials which man learned to accomplish.

But before we come down to the details, there are several wider aspects of this matter which should be mentioned. In considering this chapter and the next one, we should realize that the environment which man encounters is made up of two major elements: material things and forces, both inanimate and animate. Animals make a purely physical and instinctive adjustment to these, while man adapts himself to them in a mental way. He gradually learns about their nature, and what can and cannot be done with them. Each mental adjustment results, at length, in knowledge, and that knowledge makes the next adjustment easier and more accurate. As man comes to know the nature and qualities of things in the environment, they seem to him, and really are to him, different things from what he at first took them to be. Iron ore was nothing to the most primitive tribes; but it became something very important to savages who had learned its nature and qualities. Knowledge thus can make of the environment, which we are accustomed to think of as fixed, like " the eternal hills," something quite different from what it was prior to the acquisition of knowledge about it.

Modern man has reached a point where he has entered upon a deliberate exploration of his environment, with the object of making his adjustments to it more and more accurate. His exploration of the natural environment is natural science, which enables him to make all those marvelous adjustments, in inventions, processes, and so forth, which are characteristic of modern civilization. He has also, as we shall see later but should not fail to realize now, explored and investigated both himself and the societies in which he lives, with the object of making his social adjustments more and more accurate. This procedure is known as social science. The following chapters should give the reader an elementary idea of what there is to know about the evolution and life of human societies, and how such knowledge makes easier and more accurate men's adjustments to their fellow-men. Later still we shall come to a chapter on science in general, which will gather up the whole matter of the deliberate study of the natural and social environment and have something to say about the methods employed in that study. We turn now to the special topic of this lesson: the transformation of materials derived from nature.

One of the first materials to be shaped was stone. Over the earth, wherever there was any stone, it was broken or ground to make heads for axes, spears, and arrows. It is interesting to note, as showing man's discrimination, how generally, in countries quite separate from one another, he had settled down, as a result of experience, upon flint as the sort of material best adapted to his purposes. Flint will fracture, if properly pressed or struck, into thin, ribbon-like flakes; it does not powder up or break into irregular lumps; and the flakes are readily chipped again, by pressure or percussion, into shapes well adapted to form cutting weapons. For all the ease of flaking it, which is far greater than of grinding, flint is exceedingly hard and imperishable. Out of a similar kind of stone, obsidian, can be flaked razors whose edges are as keen as those of broken glass, but not so fragile; they are used for shaving or for other operations requiring a keen, strong blade.

The process of selection by which men arrived at the use of stone of such qualities is readily enough inferred, but the final result of experience with it is a workmanlike dexterity that modern white men have marveled at without being able to rival it. The right amount of pressure or percussion, applied at the proper spot and in the right direction, will split off the desired portion; but it takes a specialist to know just how to do it, as well as to choose stones that will not reveal flaws. Many men must have tried and failed in the acquisition of the special knowledge of nature's arrangements, and of the skill in adapting the method to the material. In the end the transformation attained an almost perfect adjustment, considering the material used, to the human need.

Another material derived from the mineral world and transformed into a human adjustment to life-conditions is iron. The high point in the use of flint came far back in the course of evolution, for in most of its important uses stone was superseded by metal long ago. In fact, the age during which the vogue of stone was at its height is often referred to as the " stone age," and what belongs to the stone age is supposed to be prehistoric. The bronze and iron ages are supposed to have succeeded the stone age and to have shown a higher culture. We shall take iron as our example of the transformation of metals, and should notice that it has not yet reached its peak of usefulness to men, though our own civilization is often said to be based upon iron.

Stone needs simply to be re-shaped; but iron must be transformed before it is worth anything to man. The metal has to be derived from the ore. One can imagine how long it took the savage to realize that there was something in the ore which was worth while, and how much longer to learn how to get it out. Although pounding will do something in extracting the metal, it takes heat to accomplish much. The great group of tribes on the American continents never learned to use iron; on the other hand, the Africans knew how to extract it from the ore, to refine it, and to work it into implements of various kinds.

The rudest way of working this metal is to heat it in an open fire, and then with stones to beat the heated mass over and over again, until the slag is removed. From this low level of effectiveness the process was gradually improved by heating the ore in underground retorts, in layers between charcoal; and the heat of combustion was heightened by a weak forced draft from a very rude type of bellows. One should consider the length of time it must have taken to arrive at the invention of the latter, for it involved the devising of valves — no small feat for primitive people. In fact, the blacksmith was commonly regarded as a wizard because of his knowledge and skill, and the metal iron as something holy and able to ward off disease and calamity. The iron horse-shoe is still so regarded in some regions.

After the metal had been brought to a sufficient purity, the African process did not differ so much from that of an old-fashioned American blacksmith, except that the latter had better tools. The African could make knives, spear-heads, hoes, and the rest of the simple implements wanted by his fellow-tribesmen, and they were of good quality. His work was necessarily slow, and he could not compete with the cheap wares of poor quality which the white trader brought. The native iron industry suffered and declined in the competition.

It is not necessary for us to rehearse the evolution of the iron industry up to the development of a steel corporation. For long ages the improvements were slow, because they were the results, very largely, of small and often chance variations, some of which were proved in the outcome to represent better adjustment to conditions. The industry came to make better products, that is, instruments which set man in better adjustment with his life-conditions.

If we content ourselves with the cases of stone and iron as illustrative of materials from the inorganic world, and turn to those drawn from the plant kingdom, the first material we think of is wood. Along with stone, it was, in all probability, among the first materials used by man. It formed the shafts of weapons whose points were of stone or bone, the handles of tools whose heads were of harder substances. The club, one of the very first instruments of man, was all of wood, and has remained so. Wood was the one material generally adapted to many purposes, because it was strong, comparatively light and easily worked, and possessed of several other qualities which will come out as we go on. Stone or metal could not begin to compare with it for most purposes of life. The expedients which a people like the Eskimo, some of whom have almost none of it, are forced to develop, give evidence as to its almost indispensable character.

As in the case of iron, where we must begin with getting the r etal from the ore, so here, we must start with getting the od from the forest. Realizing the nature of the cutting tools i savage man before he attained to metal — and we must realize that many tribes never attained to a hardened metal — it is easy for us to imagine the task of felling and trimming a large tree, to make, say, a dug-out canoe even twenty feet long. In museums it is possible to see beams five or six inches in diameter which have been cut off with stone or shell axes. Their ends look as if they had been bruised or mashed off. If cutting tools of such quality had been all that men had, the use of wood would have been held back a great deal. But all the savage tribes we know have had fire; and fire it was that opened the way in wood-working as it did in the working of iron.

The custom was to build fires around the trunk of a tree and keep them going until the trunk was charred, when the charred part could be removed with a stone axe; and the process could be repeated indefinitely. This took time; but time was precisely the one thing of which the savage had a large and sure supply. Then, when the tree was down, and it was necessary to hollow it out, that too was done by fire—the combustion being limited to the desired area by clay walls, kept drenched with water. While we are considering the working of wood by fire, we might as well mention the fact that the bending and shaping of wood was done by heat, although in this case it was heated water and steam. The dug-out was filled with water, and red-hot stones dropped in; then cross-pieces, or thwarts, were forced in, and the yielding wood spread and shaped. The bending of sticks for various purposes was done after steaming them. Where metal was known, wood was bored with red-hot rods.

Wood-working has depended in great part, however, upon the development of edged tools; thus the development of one set of adjustments is dependent upon that of another, just as that of so many, in a number of fields, has been dependent upon the control of fire. When one looks into a well-appointed carpenter's chest, and then realizes that the wood-working instruments of man before metals were of stone and bone, he wonders that they could have done so much with so little. But time and patience effected a great deal, and rubbing and scraping with stone will often accomplish in the end results that would do credit to sharp steel; and the time element is of little consequence.

The most curious piece of wood-working done by savage men — and it is performed by one of the most backward races — is the boomerang of the Australians. Other tribes have implements approaching it in its special peculiarity and which form transitional stages from a plain throwing-stick to this device, whose name has come to be a common term for anything, even a remark, which returns to strike him who hurled it. The boomerang is not so much a weapon as a toy. It is a thin, flattened, curved piece of wood, in shape not unlike what the boat-builder calls a " knee." When correctly thrown, it describes a wide circle, whirling, and also ascending and descending at various points in its flight, and returns to the neighborhood, or even to the feet, or head, of the thrower. Its peculiarity is its shape, and also the fashioning of its flattened surfaces. The choice of wood is very important; and the shape must be just right, to get the perfect result. Let one consider the number of trials and failures, and all the minute variations that must have been stumbled upon — for it takes a learned mathematician to explain the theory of the boomerang — before this odd adjustment was attained.

It would be possible to descant at some length upon the use of reeds and grasses, including as one product, for instance, the ingenious contrivance of the blow-gun. This is a bamboo or wooden pipe, through which is puffed a short, sharp dart tipped with a deadly poison — a notable adjustment, for its action is silent as well as deadly, and does not frighten away other possible victims. In the case of monkey-hunting, for instance, the monkey that is struck merely scratches a little more diligently and presently falls, which does not seem to strike his companions as particularly unnatural or indicative of danger.

There is one plant product derived out of nature and utilized by man in adjustment to the environment of microscopic enemies — Peruvian bark, or quinine — which deserves to be singled out. We do this, not because there is anything significant about the process by which this febrifuge is prepared, or for any other reason except that its discovery illustrates the blundering way in which so many important expedients have been hit upon, selected out by actual test, and transmitted — in this case as a boon to the whole world. The Indian doctor, or medicine-man, was always on the lookout for something to cure disease. But his theory of disease was that it was caused by evil spirits that had taken up their abode in the sick person's body. To effect a cure, they must be driven out, and this might be done, he thought, by some magic substance. He knew no chemistry at all, but he hunted in the dark of the moon for something to which he had no rational clue, and tried out what he found upon his patients.

In the course of time he blundered upon a number of medicines which we still use, among them the bark of the cinchona. Of course it worked when administered to a fever-patient; and he noticed this and knew he had found his magic powder. He made a great reputation and, dying, passed his secrets on to his successor. His theory was all wrong; his methods were often grotesque, for he capered about his patient, muttering charms and beating a tom-tom; but he got results. The fact that they were arrived at by accident, according to our ideas, has no bearing upon their importance. This is a specially instructive case, and will be recalled in another connection, later on. The adjustment of a man, when he has plenty of quinine, to life-conditions which include fever-bearing agencies, is not as perfect as that of the snake, which is constituted immune from fever; but it is evidently far better than it was before he possessed the febrifuge. Similarly protected, in the neighborhood of smallpox, is the person who has been vaccinated.

In considering, now, the derivation of materials from the animal world, we shall center our attention upon certain products made in good part from animal substance, instead of upon two or three animal materials alone. We refer to adjustments for bodily protection from the elements: clothing and shelter. These, along with food, constitute a sort of basic trio of human needs. It is true that they are drawn from the plant world and even from the inorganic realm, as well as from the animals; but some of the very earliest clothing is composed of skins, and the same is the case with shelter. It is to be noted that, in a large sense, clothing and houses are the same thing: the former is put upon the body, and fits closely, while the body enters the latter, which is stationary and, so to speak, fits loosely. But the service, in either case, is much the same.

The animal substances utilized for bodily protection are

chiefly hides and hair. The Eskimo uses the large bones of the whale to form a framework over which to stretch skins, so that the bones correspond to the wooden uprights and beams employed by peoples who have better resources; and he takes the split intestines of large animals to make water-proof garments. By some peoples grease or paint is employed as protection against insects, thus constituting a sort of clothing. But if we confine ourselves to the case of leather, and of fabrics made of hair or wool, we shall cover the essence of adjustments for bodily protection.

Skins of both birds and animals are made into clothing, but animal hides predominate. They are used oftentimes without removal of the hair, the hair-side being turned out or in according to special circumstances. But when the hair is removed, a special process must have been invented. It is possible to speculate on the slow and faltering steps by which knowledge of such a process developed. Then, too, the hides, unless specially treated, dry into unyielding stiffness; and the savage had to learn how to make them flexible. Untold ages ago he had learned to scrape them, removing shreds of flesh and sinew and making them thinner, and then to rub them with some softening substance, often with the brains of their former possessors. Various substances, such as certain barks, were used to tan the hides; the pores were filled up, and they were rendered water-tight. No better clothing of its sort was made than the buckskin garments of the Indians or their moccasins.

And when the skins were all prepared, there was the further necessity of cutting them to fit and sewing the pieces together. The Indian was a good tailor as well as tanner. The sewing was done with another animal product, shredded sinew, called sinnet. The tendons, or "tough-leather," were split up into fibers, and a thorn or bone awl used to punch the holes through which this sinew-thread was to pass. Seams were so cleverly made that they too were water-tight. Much of the skin clothing of the most backward peoples was not nearly so well constructed as that of the Eskimo; for the latter were much farther along the road of skillful adaptation than, for example, the African Bushman or the Fuegian. The Fuegian had merely a sort of square of skin, hung about his neck, which he shifted to windward to catch some of the snow and sleet that came his way.

Hides that were used for tents or hut-coverings were naturally of a ruder and coarser quality, and less attention was given to softening them; but those employed as coverings at night, like the " buffalo robe " of the Indians, were often of the softest and most flexible quality.

More truly " manufactured," however, were the clothes made of animal hair or wool. Camel's and alpaca's hair has been widely used in certain parts of the world, as well as the hair of goats and dogs; but the wool of the sheep is the best example of animal fiber that we meet. It is understood that what we have to say of the working-up of wool applies also to cotton and other plant fibers. Hair and wool were used long before people arrived at the point where good plant fibers were available; but in general the processes developed for one sort of material were applicable to the other.

The first of these processes was spinning, which consists in making a thread. Human beings are not adjusted, like the spider, to the making of thread; they have no organs for secreting the thread-substance and then expelling it in strands from the body. Such an endowment comes by physical evolution, while men have to invent by using their minds. The thread has to be made by twisting single hairs together; and this can be done successfully by reason of the fact that the single fibers are roughened and have microscopic hooks upon their surfaces, so that they will cling together when twisted. The simplest form of twisting is done with the thumb and finger; and sometimes the palm of the hand and the surface of the thigh are the instrumentalities employed. Later comes the spindle, a top-like instrument, which has the separate strands attached to it and is then whirled. By such methods threads of a delicate or coarser quality are made, the coarser ones running up to the size of stout fish-lines or even ropes.

When the thread is done, it is still not ready to be put on as clothing — though there are plenty of persons in the warmer zones whose whole attire consists of a string about the waist, from which various trinkets are hung. For real clothing a further development is necessary. This is weaving. Weaving with fine threads, so as to make a fabric, is the lineal descendant of weaving with coarse strands, such as reeds, rattans, or withes, by which mats or baskets are constructed. The idea of mat-weaving is to lay down a row of reeds parallel and close together, and then work other strands across, over and under, until a sort of grating is formed which holds together by reason of the fact that the elastic strands cling to one another. The same process is used in making cloth, but here there is employed an instrument called the loom. Its modern form is incredibly complicated, but the essential operations of all looms appear in the earliest and simplest forms.

The early weaver searches out a tree, let us say, which has sent out a horizontal branch not far above the ground. To this branch he ties his threads as close together as he desires, and lets them hang down. The farther apart they are, the looser and coarser the fabric will be. He now begins to work in the cross-threads, over and under; and if he wants a close fabric, he knocks each thread up with a rod against the last one. But the weaver soon found out that he could work the cross-thread in better if it had a stiff point; so he provided it with one, much as in sewing we head a thread with a needle. This developed into a shuttle. The primitive weaver did not get much farther than this; but, considering his circumstances, he had done remarkably well in his adjusting. Consider the series of more or less unconscious trials and rejections and successes that must have preceded an accomplishment which seems to us so small. If we should undertake to trace the spinning and weaving processes on up to their present stage, we should swamp the reader in masses of mechanical detail; but what the most developed machines are doing is, after all, only what the primitive weaver did: making threads and interlacing them. The process has been developed to its present high point of efficiency by the accumulation of many small variations upon the original methods and instruments, during which there has been an elimination of the inferior and a transmission of the more expedient.

The foregoing cases are no more than representative samples of man's utilization of natural materials. The point to note about them all is that they were not planned and thought out beforehand, but were happened upon, rather, in the effort to satisfy immediate needs. When we come to the place where specialists — for instance, chemists — are deliberately exploring nature for new materials and elements, such as synthetic rubber or radium, we have arrived at a very modern and advanced stage of things. We must not carelessly assume that the savage did anything of that sort; it is not at all justifiable to carry back into the earlier and simpler stages the ideas and theories of a highly complicated culture. Enlightenment comes from starting at the other end: finding out the facts about the simpler forms of adjustment and then following the evolutionary series up toward its latest forms.

CHAPTER V

THE APPROPRIATION OF FORCES

There exist in nature a number of forces, such as gravitation, to which all organic beings must adjust. Animals do this in their usual instinctive way; but it is characteristic of men that they have learned actual. to use these forces, systematically, in the promotion of human well-being. For instance, the force of gravitation is enlisted in the pile-driver, and the force of expanding gas in the steam-engine. The types of energy shown in nature have been classified into those of the inanimate and the animate world. An example of the former is the elasticity of steel; of the latter, the pulling-power of the horse. Forces from the animate world may be divided into non-human and human. Of course, one of the greatest forces in the world is man himself; and his energies are both physical and mental. We shall cover, in this chapter, examples of energies derived from the inanimate world, from animals, and from men.

Looked at from another angle, the types of natural energy have been classified into (1) mechanical energies; (2) heat; (3) light; (4) electric and magnetic energies; and (5) chemical energies. We shall give our space to the chemical energies alone. Of mechanical energies, falling water and the flow of the tides form good examples. Heat and light need not be considered by themselves, as they are caused by chemical action. Electric and magnetic energies belong to a later age than the others, for the latter had been long in use before the former became available to man. The chemical energies are the most manifold of all; for each of the multitude of different forms of matter exhibits its own type of chemical energy, and combinations are always yielding new types. Organisms, whether plants, animals, or human beings, depend for their activities exclusively upon chemical energy. Life itself is based upon chemical materials and processes. Food is a set of chemical substances which are transformable into cell-material, and so into the bodily structure of living things. We might even have put the food-quest under the present topic.

Interest centers, first, in the employment by man, in his effort to live, of the natural forces of the inanimate world. He has had great successes in so doing, with his wind-mills, gas-engines, and dynamos; and he sometimes gets to thinking that he can not only control nature, but even create things out of nothing. It is an obvious fact, however, when one stops to think of it, that he can never alter natural laws. He can arrange a situation so that some natural force will work unimpeded; or he can oppose one force to another. He can grease the ways at a launching, so that gravitation may draw a ship into the water; or he can roughen the ways so that gravitation is opposed and defeated by friction. He has to take the natural forces as they are, and adjust himself to their laws. He can make no new laws for them.

His successes are in direct proportion to his knowledge of the various unchanging ways of nature, for it is that knowledge which enables him to make such adjustments as will allow him to live, or to live better. The race has always been deeply interested in the story of successes so won, especially under novel and trying circumstances. One of the classic stories in English literature is that of Robinson Crusoe who, when thrown into a strange environment, succeeded in adjusting himself by cleverness in sizing up the situation and meeting it.

One of the first forces in nature which men appropriated was fire. No tribes have been found who did not have it, though there are some who are careful not to let it go out, because their methods of re-kindling are faulty. The probability is that men got it originally from conflagrations kindled by lightning, and that the development of methods of generating it came much later. The simplest of these methods was the friction-process, in which two sticks were rubbed together in a variety of ways; and later came the percussion-process in which sparks were struck from stone and caught in tinder.

It would be a long story to recount the utilities of fire to mankind. We have noted that fire is usually at the basis of any form of manufacture; and that is perhaps the utility which seems to us, in this age, the most important of all. But it was not so in the childhood of the race. To the savage the greatest service of fire was probably the scaring-off, by its heat and light, of the evil spirits by which he fancied himself surrounded. We shall return to this point when we consider primitive religious ideas. If we seek to get to the very bottom of the matter, we meet one fact of the highest importance, namely, that there are many countries where men could not live were it not for fire. This puts fire into the same class, as an adjustment, with the layer of blubber or the coat of fur developed by animals in cold climates. It is difficult to see how, without fire, any parts of the earth outside the tropics could have been settled. But we have learned that civilization is a product of regions lying outside the hot belt. So that we might conclude that without fire there could not have been such civilization as has been developed in temperate regions alone.

It is evident enough that the warmth and also the light of his oil-lamps are what enable the Eskimo to live in the far north; but it is also true, though perhaps less obvious, that early man, in whatever region he lived, secured a necessary protection in that heat and light. Wild animals, including serpents, scorpions, and insects in general, are repelled by the flame and smoke; the smudge is still used against the winged insects. The typical savage dwelling portrayed in stories — and the stories are not all fanciful — is a cave with a fire burning in or just outside the opening. Thus equipped, the savage was safe from most attacks of his animal competitors, especially at night when the danger was greatest. No other single form of protection approaches fire in its efficacy.

The use of heat in the cooking of food was also an adjustment of the first importance in living. Among the rudest savages who cook their food, the eating of meat in a raw state is looked upon as a mark of bestiality, and peoples who practise it are called, in great contempt, " Raw-eaters." The softening of food and the breaking up of the food-cells, by heat, certainly lightens the strain of digestion, and frees energy employed in a merely animal process so that it can be applied to better advantage. Further, heat and smoke are preservatives, and the preservation of food against the future is one of the first exhibitions of that prime virtue of civilization, foresight.

We have seen that fire is a sort of indispensable tool in the working of wood and metal. It is also a weapon; for it is frequently used in hunting, to drive the game upon the spears of the hunters. It is employed in signaling, and constitutes the primitive telegraph. By its use pottery is baked, land is cleared and fertilized, and sacrifices offered to the gods. The fire-place is the center of the home, as the altar is of the temple. One does not wonder, as he reflects over the many and important uses of fire, that many peoples have been fire-worshippers. We stand here before one of the most indispensable and successful adjustments that men have ever made in living. No animal ever arrived at it, and men attained it so long ago that all trace of its discovery is lost. As usual in such cases, it was accredited to the gods.

Fire might be considered as a force derived out of the inorganic world. To it might be added the expansive and explosive forces of gases which have rendered possible the engines, guns, and other instrumentalities, many of which are dependent on the ignition of gases — thus going back again in part to fire. Consider also the electric battery, in which, by bringing together certain inorganic substances — copper, zinc, and sulphuric acid, for instance — a new power, electricity, is developed from which, again, are derived heat and light. Consider the advantage to human life of the utilization of coal and its various products. But all such developments are so modern that they scarcely belong in this sketch of the beginnings of the several forms of adjustment.

Fire may stand as a typical case of the appropriation of force from the inanimate realm. Perhaps the best example of the derivation of power out of the organic world is the domesticated animal. The topics of domestication and breeding, however, have already been summoned before the reader's attention and need not be rehearsed; but we should recall the additions to man's strength and speed represented, for instance, by the ox and horse. Without the reindeer and the dog the peoples of the extreme north could scarcely maintain life; without the camel desert tribes might well cease to exist; without the great strength of the ox or horse real agriculture is hardly possible.

There is another force that men have derived out of the organic world, and that is the physical power of other men. In order to utilize this, the system of slavery was developed — not planned out deliberately, but gradually worked into, through a series of variations. At first all prisoners were killed — often tortured to death; then women and children were kept and used, much as if they were domestic animals; and finally grown men were enslaved. By this method the physical forces in the slaves were at the disposal of the masters, and the life of the latter was rendered so much the more satisfactory to them. To some extent the masters were able also to appropriate the mental powers of the slaves; but the great failure of slave labor has always been due to the fact that the slave had no driving interest to better himself, but worked simply from fear. This meant that he did not put his mind and its energy into what he was doing; that is, the masters did not really succeed in appropriating his mental energies. Slavery was a good adjustment in its day. It got work done that would not have been done without it. But it could never compete with free labor and was gradually selected away in the competition, for it had become a maladjustment. For long ages of evolution it persisted, and there was no objection to it; in the Bible, for instance, it is not condemned; but under changing conditions it failed at length to stand the pace, fell into disrepute, came under moral condemnation, and was abolished.

If a system like slavery fails to utilize the mental as well as the physical energies of men, there are other adjustments which both free those energies and also stimulate them. In general, it is emotion rather than reason which forms the mainspring to human action; and emotion is rooted in wants, or, more broadly, in interests. To get action from human beings, the method approved by experience is an appeal to interest. It is only when we approach the matter from this angle that we come to realize how many social arrangements are adjustments to human wants, and are so ordered as to appeal to them and arouse them. Human wants are manifold, and are never satisfied; for new wants grow out of the satisfaction of old ones, without end.

There are certain basic needs and interests, appeals to which may be found in the social system of any people. First of all, any man needs a *chance* if he is to put forth all his energies. In the case of slavery, the difficulty is that the slave cannot get ahead, however much he puts into his work. That kills his interest and quells all ambition. What he needs to stimulate him to the output of energy is a chance to satisfy his wants. It is not so much the satisfaction itself as the chance to get the satisfaction that will move him; for if satisfaction is handed out gratis, there is no stimulus to put forth effort. Suppose, however, that the slave is allowed to profit somewhat personally from extra effort — to accumulate some property or even to own a wife; then the situation is entirely changed, and he is moving over toward the system of free labor which, in the end, has proved itself so superior to slavery.

The basic want of man is to live, and he cannot display much energy if his chances of seeing tomorrow are small. Nothing can be got out of him while he is in terror of his life, for he is preoccupied. He needs to be released from that fear and apprehension. To meet this need, society has developed the institutions that secure law and order. In a country possessing such safeguards to life, much more human force is appropriated to the welfare of all than in a lawless and anarchistic society. But the assurance of mere existence — the right to life — is not going very far. Men want to live better. They will struggle and put forth effort to do so if they see a chance to benefit by it. If a society can assure a man that no one will take away what he gets, or interfere with him in the getting of it for himself and family, his powers will be set free and his ambition stimulated. Compare the power elicited from the people of this country, especially in its earlier days, with the amount derived from a population which is hampered and limited, as in Russia, under a system which allows constant interference with personal liberty — especially if that population has a good share or all of its winnings taken away in the form of heavy taxes. Freedom and security mean copious opportunity.

It is not to be understood that all can have freedom at the same time, without any limitation. If I am not to be interfered with by my neighbor, that means that freedom to interfere with me is denied to him; and also that I am not warranted in getting in his way or picking his pockets. No one is absolutely free, in a human society; for we must all get along together, and nobody may do exactly as he pleases. Our liberty is liberty under law; and what the law does is, at its best, and theoretically, to allow everyone all the freedom possible consistently with granting everyone else the same. The line has to be drawn somewhere, and someone is always dissatisfied — the thief is not content with what most of us regard as a proper arrangement. Nor will the line stay drawn as life-conditions change, but must be corrected and adjusted over and over again as human circumstances alter. In England the death-penalty used once to be visited upon the theft of goods worth more than a few pence; now even the theft of thousands of dollars belonging to widows and orphans is not so punished. In fact, it looks sometimes as if theft on the small scale is now punished where theft on the large scale once was. But the laws, at least in theory, aim to limit everyone as little as possible — that is, to assure everyone the greatest freedom — consistent with the interest of all.

Where this is done with some degree of success, human powers are set free, and society profits by it just as by the appropriation of animal energies out of nature. Through many ages, and with much groping and variation, the process of freeing human energy has been going on; and at every stage social arrangements and institutions have been evolved corresponding to the stage attained by the process. One of the best ways to find out what people want, and let them get it, is to free public opinion. Once the despot had the say about nearly everything and his opinion was the governing factor, unless he became too arbitrary and was assassinated. But now the idea is to let everyone talk, and to decide as to policy on the basis of a general expression of opinion at stated times, in an election. Between the two forms of despotism and democracy there is a long evolution, into which we shall not now seek to penetrate.

Opportunity assured to individual ambition, together with freedom in dealing with it, has been found, in history, to be the great liberator and stimulus to strong and sustained effort. But those who put forth the energy must be allowed to enjoy its fruits. Any system which has sought to equalize everybody's gains by taking away from the efficient to give to the inefficient, has been as bad or worse than one which frankly robbed some to enrich others, with no theory of human brotherhood to cloak such inexpediency. One is as poor an adjustment as the other; only there was some reason for the frank robbery of former centuries, whereas, in the light of history, there is no excuse for the leveling propositions of today. Nothing that discourages individual initiative and dampens the ardor of human energies can be well for society.

Freedom to reap the rewards of effort makes a strong appeal to human interests and emotions, and stimulates the output of human energy. So does the call to patriotism. It is often unreasonable or sensational; but that makes no difference. Patriotism is a sentiment that any nation needs to nourish all it can, though " My country, right or wrong " is not a pleasing phrase to a thoughtful man. The very persistence of a nation depends upon the rallying of its citizens to its defense in time of peril; and the appeal to patriotism, if successful, rouses tremendous human force. A state is better adjusted to its life-conditions if its citizens are susceptible to that appeal, just as any smaller team of men is more powerful if it has a " spirit." Consequently the various devices to encourage patriotism, such as the flag, the national holiday and anthem, traditions of the Founders, accounts of the nation's prowess, all represent adjustments calculated to evoke power.

One of the strongest interests of man lies in his vanity. Much of patriotism, indeed, is national vanity. The individual can be led to put forth greater energy, perhaps, in the satisfaction of vanity than in any other way. Flattery has been not only one of the most obvious methods of stimulating energy, but also one of the most subtle. The prospect of winning renown has stimulated to superhuman efforts many a man who was unassailable through the grosser forms of appeal to a grosser vanity. In adjustment to this deep-seated characteristic, all societies have evolved prizes to be striven for; and perhaps those offered to the savage are, comparatively speaking, more numerous and alluring than any that are dangled before the eyes of civilized man. The latter has his badges, ribbons, uniforms, coronets, eulogies, offices, and publicity of all kinds, and he strives mightily to get them; but there is an even greater stimulus exerted upon the Malay or the Indian.

First of all, there is the deepest humiliation in not acquiring the distinguishing prize. No young fellow, among many savage tribes, can become a man until he gets some trophy, or endures some ordeal, or otherwise proves himself. Until he does that, his manhood is " not proven"; for age alone will not do that. He may not marry, and, since a wife is the mark of a man, he does not belong among the warriors. In fact, if he fails in his tests, he must go back and live among the women and children, as heretofore, and have no account taken of him. He may not join the secret society; he becomes the butt of everybody, especially of the girls, who constantly jeer at him; and his life is little short of intolerable.

What a boy is supposed to do is to endure, without a whimper but smiling, the painful lacerations and tortures that have been devised to test his courage. He must kill his man and get a skull or scalp as a trophy, or perform some other exploit that proves him a hunter or a warrior of parts. If he passes through this ordeal with credit, he may then be gashed or tattooed, as becomes a man, or have some of his teeth knocked out, or have his lips or ears bored, or be otherwise marked as an adult. Then he may marry, belong to the secret society, attend the councils, and otherwise enter into his majority. The amount of effort and endurance which boys show in going through these ceremonies is truly incredible; some of them die under it. And if one fails the first time and the whole thing is repeated, the succeeding test is no less severe.

For the sake of mere decoration, savage men and women will endure the protracted agonies of a wholesale tattooing or of a deformation of the foot. In order to appear holy and inspire reverence, the Hindu fanatic will lie smiling on a bed of spikes. To get into the secret societies, men will work and save until they can pay the initiation fee. To become a noted warrior, with many feathers, each indicative of an exploit or " coup," the Indian will practise and endure hardship unswervingly. To become a medicine-man, a young fellow will go through fastings and beatings and tortures especially devised to test his capabilities for that eminent and lucrative office.

One of the strongest sentiments in savage man is ghost-fear, or terror before the supernatural. The appeal to that emotion has always been one of the strongest provocatives to action. Primitive religion is full of demands on time and energy which no one dare refuse, and which amount to the eliciting of effort that would not otherwise be put forth. Capital must be gathered somehow to pay for sacrifices, to buy welfare in the world to come, and to fee the medicine-man for protection from evil influences, not only for the individual himself, but for his crops, his beasts, and all the rest of his possessions. This is a long story, only to be hinted at here; but the reader of mediæval history knows well how effort and wealth were expended for or drifted into the hands of the priests in order to secure welfare in the world to come. Consider the amount of toil and capital that was sunk in the construction of tombs like the Pyramids. Fear of the supernatural has been appealed to by all religions, and it has stirred men to action in all ages. It has evoked power, that is to say, where power would not have been evoked but for this special appeal.

All these social arrangements that were calculated to call forth human energy in greater amount were devised by nobody in particular. They were hit upon as variations in the ways of living, proved their efficiency in the fact, and became customary. Every human society, in savagery or in civilization, drifted into much the same methods of tapping surplus human energy, and, when it did so, profited by it just as if it had acquired another extra energy out of nature. All the instrumentalities hit upon for evoking such extra energy plainly constitute adjustments to life-conditions; and the more successfully they operate the more fit is the society in the competition with other societies. We must keep this matter of adjustment constantly to the fore, even though it seems to be wearisomely insisted upon; for it is the key to the whole matter of the development of society's ways, customs, and institutions.

CHAPTER VI

PROPERTY AND PROPERTY-RIGHTS

When men had appropriated materials out of nature, or had domesticated animals or plants, or had enslaved men, we find that such things were regarded as belonging to some person or persons. They were somehow attached to him or them. In some cases the bond was an actual one, as where an amulet was hung about its owner's neck; again it was not a material bond at all, but was, as one might say, an invisible attachment, as when a man owned a cow. This invisible bond was about as strong as an actual one. Such a connection between a person and a thing, whereby the thing is attributed to or set aside for the person, is a property-tie, and the thing is known as property.

The development of property is an adjustment whereby desirable objects derived out of nature are distributed in such manner that there is a minimum of quarreling and fighting over them. Everyone wants these objects because he can live better if he has them, and it is necessary to have some rules about who has and who has not, for generally all cannot have or use a thing at the same time. Where that is possible, as in the case of the air, there is no property; among simple peoples water also is generally as " free as air." It is not at all to be understood that men thought these matters out; they experienced the ills resulting from greed and quarrels and struck out on various lines of action to avoid those ills, arriving at length at the development of the property-idea. The essence of that idea is that all others shall hold off and let the owner or owners have his or their objects undisturbed.

Hence the very germ of property lies in holding a thing against all others, that is, in monopoly. If there were no property-system, still everyone would try to hold what he had against all others; and all would also be trying to get what each had away from him. Men have always quarreled over property a great deal, system or no system; but society, for its own self-preservation, has had to minimize this strife so far as it could by guaranteeing possession, that is, by prohibiting and punishing theft. " Thou shalt not steal " is one of the universal rules for life in society.

To uphold a property-right there is need of force. Once the strong man could take away what the weak had and hold it so long as he remained strong. This is still seen among children, who are chronically primitive and lawless in their ideas until they learn better. And when the weak man can hold property in the face of a strong rival, that is because behind the weaker is the whole force of the tribe, with which no one person, however strong, is able to cope. If a person steals nowadays, it is a representative of the community at large who arrests him and another who condemns him to punishment. And if the local authorities are not strong enough, the state's forces and, in the end, the national army and navy can be called in. There is always plenty of force behind the property-bond. Men have never been in greater earnest about anything than about the safeguarding of property-rights. And why not? Property is provision for life and comfort, and a man will surrender it only after all defense has failed. It can be seen that property-arrangements are very deep-seated affairs, and not likely to be changed over night.

Property-systems begin with things that are relatively scarce, and the scarcer they are the more intense is the feeling about their ownership. It follows that whatever becomes scarce is likely to become property; thus in a city the water-supply belongs to certain owners, who sell it to consumers, whereas an Indian village on a river bank does not recognize property in water. If at a hotel one pays more for an outside room, he is probably paying for sunlight and air, which were once free. Thus property, in its evolution, comes to cover things not originally included. Again, certain things may be desirable as property to some people and not to others; for instance, the iron and coal deposits in America did not interest the Indians at all, though they now form properties of great desirability and value. The Eskimo who traded some fine furs for a handful of wet matches with red sticks, was eager to own what the white man was just about to throw away as useless.

Another fact that should be noted is that the use of a thing is not equivalent to property-right in it. What is sometimes called common property, like a town green or common, is owned by no individual, though he may have the right to use it for certain purposes. When native people have sold land to white men, they have sometimes thought they were merely selling the use of that land, for a season of planting and harvesting, and have been very much surprised and disgusted when they have discovered that the white men meant to hold the land as their own property right along. Then have come attack, resistance, and bloodshed.

There have been contradictory assertions about early forms of property, some persons holding that all property was originally held in common, and others that it was all private. Neither assertion is universally true; the fact is that some things were held one way and some the other, depending on the nature of the things. Thus, again, these forms of property-holding are adjustments to life-conditions. Some have said that all movable objects were held as private property and all immovables as common. That statement of the case is nearer the truth. But it is still more exact to say that generally those things were held in common which the individual had no object in owning, but of which everyone wanted to use. Weapons and tools could not well be owned in common, nor could an ornament, or a charm, or clothing, or anything else that the individual carried or wore. Such things were attached to him pretty closely and could not well be shared. On the other hand, the house and its furnishings, being for common use, were often regarded as family-property, just as they are now; for the home is referred to as " our " house, even though the father or the mother owns it, or even, indeed, though it be rented from some other owner. This is not always true among savages, however, for often the household belongings are strictly divided into the husband's and the wife's. Sometimes the head of the family appears as the owner of what is really common property, just as the chief may be spoken of as the owner of a tribe's possessions.

Whatever the arrangement, it always appears as a local adjustment, generally pretty well suited to allow of living without disputes. There are some tribes, and they are all backward peoples, who have what is virtually common property in food; that is, anyone has the right to share in whatever anyone else gets. Any such tribesmen cannot understand how people could starve to death while others had food, and asks, " Why do they not go and eat with their neighbors? " The result of this sharing practice is that the worthless get along by living on the energetic and ambitious, and that energy and ambition are not long in either being extinguished or in evading the custom in some manner. Anything that reduces men to an equality of this sort will soon reduce them to an equality at zero. It is significant that instances of such practice are to be found only among undeveloped peoples; any policy of artificially equalizing the possessions of all aims squarely at a return to uncivilization. Men are unequal; and it is well that they are, for otherwise there would be no variation to start off the process of adjustment; and any scheme for ignoring this natural and obvious truth must work out into maladjustment to the facts and conditions of human life.

The simplest case to illustrate the evolution of property-forms as adjustments to life-conditions is that of ownership of land. Land is needed, one might say, as a place to stand on, or in which to be buried; but there has always been enough standing-room for everyone, on the primitive stage, and the dead have usually been disposed of in such manner as not to occupy soil that living men might want. In general, it has not been the land itself — the dirt — that has been of interest to men. A deposit of clay, or flint, or salt, or of some metal, has been desirable, and men have fought over such things; but the chief and all-pervading interest in land has been, not in the land itself, but in the organic life connected with the land. For this has been the food-supply, as well as the source of clothing and other protection for the body. Land has served for a hunting-ground, a grazing-ground, and a tillage-area, and as it has passed through this series the form in which it has been held as property has adjusted nicely to life-conditions.

Among hunters there is no reason why any particular person should want any particular area of land as his own. The game does not stay in one place; in fact, it would be better for a man to own certain pools in the streams than a small area of land. What everyone wants is the right to hunt over a large area; and when he has hunted it over, he is done with it for the time. He does not care to keep others off it when he is not there. He has no special interest in any small fraction of it; what he wants is the use, not the ownership or monopoly, of it. There is no call for private ownership, that is, on the hunting stage. But every tribe is interested in keeping all others off its common hunting-ground, or food-preserve. Savages are strict about this, and designate the bounds of their hunting-grounds by natural landmarks, such as rivers, boulders, and large trees. When an alien tribesman comes to such boundaries, he knows it is dangerous to pass them without permission; for the tribe which is in possession will defend its monopoly with vigor.

It can be said, then, that the tribe owns the hunting-ground, which is used in common. This is about what is meant by common or communal property in land. The whole tribe owns its hunting-ground, and its right to that property in land lies in its power to hold it against all other tribes. But in most cases what is in the mind is the possible food that is ranging over the country, and also the fuel that is growing upon it. If the game fails, the land is abandoned as worthless; and the Indian hunters had the fuel question so firmly in mind that, when asked why they thought the whites had come to America, replied that doubtless their wood-supply had failed and they were looking for a country better stocked with trees.

People who have advanced to domestication of animals show scarcely more interest in land as land than the hunters do. What they want, above all, is food for their flocks and herds. But no individual wants to be confined to some one restricted area for grazing purposes; he wants the use of wide ranges. As soon as the grass is all gone from any piece of land, the land is of no further use and is abandoned. Cattle-raisers are constant wanderers, passing from pasture to pasture with the seasons and leaving the areas behind them completely stripped of everything valuable to them. Consider the Huns and their migrations. When sheep have grazed over a piece of land, there is not much there for any other grass-eating animal. And so, on this stage too, there is a general and common use of all the pasture there is by everyone in the herding tribe, together with a tribal monopoly of the area in use as against other tribes. No call for private ownership appears, and private property does not develop as an adjustment to the situation.

It is to be understood that we are dealing in types and generalities when we draw such a conclusion. As a matter of fact, there may be circumstances which, even among hunters, lead to private property in land, or something approaching it. For instance, an Indian woman used to own, sometimes, a grove of maple trees as a sugar-camp; and occasionaly we find that a tribal hunting-ground is parcelled out to heads of families, so that it becomes really communal family-property. The idea in the latter case was to preserve the game, that is, to counteract the general communal system wherein no one was responsible for economy in killing the animals. This provision or adjustment reveals one of the inherent weaknesses of any communal system — the lack of individual responsibility. What is the business of all is the business of none. So long as game is as plentiful as it used to be on the plains of the American West there was no call for care in dealing with it; but as soon as there was such a call, then the responsibility had to be put up definitely to a few, and not vaguely to all. That is, the old system of common property was turning into a maladjustment.

On the herding stage, too, there were departures from the general type, as sketched above. Old towns, even in this country, sometimes have a "common," where once the beasts were pastured, so that common property went along with private holdings in cultivated land; and the so-called "waste" was for the use of all. But pasture-land has often come to be enclosed and privately owned, especially where the whole livelihood was not derived from the herds but where there were comparatively few animals owned. These departures from the typical herding arrangements, where the herds were almost the sole source of livelihood, only emphasize the element of variation and reveal a changing adjustment harmonizing with changing life-conditions.

It is when we come to tillage that the typical property-system as respects land undergoes a decided change. Even the maple-grove case is a sort of agricultural or orchard affair; and the modification of pasture-holding is generally in connection with agriculture, where fewer animals are owned. Under agriculture the whole situation as respects land is altered. It is still the product of the land rather than the land itself that is the object of desire; but now some small areas of land are better than others, whereas on the hunting and herding stages there was small choice between limited plots. One piece of tillage-land is, perhaps, naturally more fertile than another, even though the two are small and lie side by side. But tillage-land must generally have been improved, by being cleared of trees and underbrush and otherwise prepared for cultivation, and sometimes enriched with ashes, fish, or other fertilizer. When this has been done, the holder of such land is not willing to give it up for any other piece; especially if the ground contains seed which he has planted, does it become a special and individual thing, of which he wants the private monopoly.

The improver of soil is not going to be content with the mere use of it. At first, when the effort and capital which he puts into it is slight, he may care to hold it only while the crop is maturing; but the more it is transformed by his hand, the more firmly he will hold to it, just as he holds to other things which he has taken out of nature and transformed, such as his bow and arrows. If he plants such long-time crops as vines and trees, which will often not ful y mature while he lives, he wants to hold the land that bea s them all his life, and then be able to bestow it as he wills. As distinguished from waste land, the sort he has made is scarce, and scarcity of a thing means that the property-right to it is intensified. Not only that; hunters and herders wander about a good deal, and cannot very well, even if they wanted to, stay and hold a section of land; but the agriculturist is sedentary, and can.

In short, on the agricultural stage the whole situation calls for the adjustment of individual ownership, or private property, in land; and the adjustment promptly appears. There was no general occasion for it before and it appeared only in isolated cases, under special circumstances. Now it comes in as a prevalent type of land-holding. And it will be noted that the welfare of the whole society is served by it. If a man may not own, for himself and his, a piece of land which he has improved, then there is no incentive to improve it. If land is to be re-distributed presently, some one else will enjoy the results of his activity. In such case the activity will not be put forth; for it is not in human nature to spend effort on that which is not one's own for the sake of those who are not one's own. To stimulate men to their best endeavors they must be assured of the fruits of those endeavors. Attempts to divide equally the products of effort that has been put forth unequally were counter to all that we know about human nature; and it has always been a disastrous, though popular policy, to rob some for the support of others. Whatever the sentimentalist may say about the beauty of altruism, the way to get results, so far as the evidence of history goes — and that is about all the real evidence we have — is to assure to each the reward of his abilities and efforts. In any case, the system of private property, in things and in land, has gone along with the development of civilization; and anyone who proposes to abolish it forthwith in favor of some sharing or communal system is suggesting a return to something long ago given up as a maladjustment. He might as well propose the abolition of monogamous marriage and of the family; for certainly they are flagrant cases of the most absolute monopoly. To say that some future change in life-conditions might call for the communalization of property is to indulge in fruitless guesswork.

One of the important developments in connection with property is inheritance. The family held together in their living as a unit; in fact, the members of a family, the dead as well as the living, constituted a close community united by the bond of a common blood. That community was held responsible for the actions of its members, to the extent that vengeance was wreaked almost indiscriminately on any member of the community for the misdeeds of any other member. And there was a strong feeling that the possessions of all dead members belonged to the rest, as next in order. What the deceased owned was sent along with him, in good part, to the spirit-world — that is, it was burned with the corpse at the funeral

or otherwise destroyed — and there was often considerable re-
luctance to take over the property of the dead, lest his ghost
should return in quest of it. Sometimes this resulted in the en-
richment of the priest or medicine-man, who was not so much
afraid of ghosts because he could use supernatural powers
against them. The priesthood generally got a good share of
the possessions of the dead, in any case, as fees for medical
attendance and for easing passage to the next life.

Nevertheless, as time went on, a person's property, in part
or as a whole, came to be transferred, at his death, to his next
of kin; and, although parents and brothers inherited to some
extent, the tendency was to pass it over to the next generation.
When relationship was reckoned, as it was among a number of
primitive tribes, exclusively through the mother, the nephew
inherited from his mother's brother. His father and his
father's kinsmen were not related to him. More commonly
the son inherited from the father, for blood-relationship of
father and son came to be accepted quite generally. Daughters
were regularly left out of account; and among the sons it was
the eldest who, as the most mature and best able to protect
the property, was most commonly the heir. There are
numerous variations in systems of inheritance, but the basic
sense of them is that property is held together and transmitted
to the next generation. And this is done in some accepted
way, so that the quarrels sure to arise over ownerless possessions do not develop to injure the stability of society. By a
system of inheritance the title to property is made continuous
even in the eventuality of the owner's death.

By it also the accumulation of capital has been rendered
less difficult. Such accumulation may not be an unmixed advantage in our age; but in the earlier stages of evolution it
meant that the younger generation could stand on the
shoulders of the older, and did not have to start from the
ground anew. It did not matter then so much as it does now
that the bulk of property lay in a few hands; the existence of

any accumulation at all was an advantage to society, just as was the fact that labor was accomplished, even under a system of slavery, rather than not done at all.

Property is a sort of explosive, the employment of which, in the interest of everybody concerned, needs to be hedged about with much restriction. It must not be left lying around, ownerless. This fact is recognized in the many customs and regulations touching upon ownership, which have developed gradually and without any premeditation throughout history. They represent expedient adjustments in the face of what might be, without them, a situation fraught with peril to society's existence. By such regulations the individual is freed from the necessity of guarding his possessions on all occasions, though he is at the same time restricted from trying to get those of others away by violent means. The interest in property forms a powerful engine, which, controlled and directed aright, has been turned into the service of society. No way has ever been found of removing from the hearts of men the interest in property. If an existing property-system becomes maladjusted, new variations of all kinds appear; but in the end the main lines of the institution are not altered. It has been too long under test to have failed to acquire, in its correspondence to age-long life conditions, a reason for being and a toughness of fiber calculated to withstand all serious assaults. When alterations have evolved, they have been those of detail rather than of general structure.

It is not meant to assert that anything human is changeless and eternal; but that when an arrangement like property or religion has survived through ages of conflict and competition, and has proved an indispensable incentive to the development of civilization, then, while it conceivably may sometime be selected away, the balance of probability is strongly in favor of its persistence — so strongly, indeed, that to the discreet any proposition to abolish it must, to receive attention, assume a tremendous burden of proof.

CHAPTER VII

EXCHANGES

In the development of civilization the exchange of materials and of ideas has been of an importance second only to their origination. For by exchange all the new departures that have turned out well for their originators have been transmitted to other peoples, back and forth; and each of several communicating groups has been able to profit by a set of adjustments which include the best that any and all of them have succeeded in hitting upon. It is a truth speedily revealed to study and reflection that men must work together in considerable numbers in order that civilization may be developed. This implies, as a prime essential, the need of intercommunication. Men must not only know what is going on in the minds of other men, so as to compare and mutually adopt ideas, but, still more important, especially among backward tribes which can most readily deal with ideas that are embodied in things, they must be able to see and handle those things—in this case, other people's products. They can communicate by speech or writing; but they must also bring products to each other; and to do that they must learn to overcome distance. This calls for transportation of men and things. And when they get into proximity, they must have some method of peaceably exchanging their products; hence the mechanism of trade, including money, measures and weights, credit, and other commercial devices. They must, further, make their products desirable to one another; hence the methods of appeal, chiefly by suggestion, practised by the trader.

All these are adjustments in the art of living, comparable with the invention of tools and weapons. We shall first note

some of the agencies for the exchange of ideas and then those
for the exchange of products. The latter predominate on the
earlier stages of development. It should not be understood,
however, that hard and fast lines of distinction can be drawn
between these two forms of exchange; the transfer of products
is hardly possible without a simultaneous transmission of
ideas, for the products are themselves ideas expressed in
material form.

First come the adjustments in communication. The prime
instrumentality for the exchange of anything between human
beings is language. We have noted that language is not a
natural endowment, but an acquired instrument. It is not inherited, but learned. It might be called a tool, without stretch-
ing that term out of all recognition; it is, at any rate, no organic product, but a social one. Its first form was doubtless
communication by gestures and signs; but we shall leave that
out of account here, and deal only with spoken language. Two
persons, speaking to one another, give an exhibition which, but
for the fact that one is so used to it, would strike him as being
quite as marvelous as "wireless." One person begins to move
his mouth and tongue, thus re-shaping certain air-waves from
his vocal chords, vibrations which are carried to beat upon a
small drum in the side of the other person's head. These beats
are carried by a series of bones and nerve-fibres to the hearer's
brain, and behold! he knows the thoughts in the speaker's
mind. This marvel, by familiarity with it, has become a
matter of course.

A further amazing fact about such communication is that
a series of customary sounds, selected and arranged by nobody,
should form a speech or language which has a regular, logical,
and complicated structure of its own. Not all languages have
the same structure, but, whatever the type, it is as fully subject
to law as are the movements of the planets. Language did not
leap to an elaborate and logical structure, with all the parts of
speech distinct, at once; it developed gradually, through varia-

tion, selection, and transmission, in adjustment to needs. It furnishes one of the best cases of evolution in the social field. Nobody made it; and everybody made it. The creation of a new language is impossible for any man, and always has been; so-called creations of new languages have simply combined old models. Yet the various languages grew, as our own is now growing, by gradual and often almost imperceptible changes. Language is evidently the handiwork of a *people*; and the rest of human institutions are that also, though we are often deceived into thinking otherwise.

An allied agency for the transmission of culture is writing. Beginning with pictures of objects, men gradually worked out to an alphabet by abbreviating and conventionalizing their drawings, and finally assigning to each character a sound that had been prominent in the name of the object originally pictured. The great service of writing has consisted in the preservation and transmission of ideas and culture across time. Its value as an adjustment can be appreciated by reflecting as to whether or not a society is better adjusted to its life-conditions if it possesses a record of the experiences and adaptations of the past. Writing also brings together those who are separated in space as well as in time; and, if printing is taken to be a developed form of writing, it establishes exchanges of the most regular and copious description. Here too is one of the marvels which are not recognized as such because of familiarity with them; that a few scratches on a chip may convey a message is regarded by the savage as a piece of powerful magic, which awes and frightens him.

In the modern age, literature discharges an important function in acquainting peoples with one another's characteristics. Perhaps the novel is as effective an instrumentality along this line as any other. For instance, in the work of Turgenev, a Russian novelist of the highest worth, there is a sort of revelation of the Russian character, in some of its most important aspects, at any rate; and the reader has no excuse, after reading Turgenev, for picturing all Russians as fierce, hairy, uncouth creatures, clad in sheepskins. Novels have portrayed the life of rural England, of the American West, of the Latin Quarter, and even of central Africa with such vividness that the reader feels that he knows, in some degree, the people and their ways.

Exchange of ideas has been the dominant note thus far in this chapter; and we wish to enforce it by one more type of illustration before turning to the exchange of material objects. Ideas can be exchanged by the exchange of human beings. In the early days this was accomplished by exogamy (marrying outside one's tribe or community), by slavery, and by trade. If one tribe got its wives from another, evidently the women would carry with them most of the adjustments which their native communities had learned to make, and would transmit them to their new fellow-tribesmen. Thus would each tribe come to possess the culture of all the intermarrying tribes. The members of all communities married fellow-members at first (endogamy), but gradually those groups which began to marry out prevailed; and one of the reasons for this, if not the main reason, was that exogamy was a better adjustment than endogamy, in that it promoted exchanges of culture. Enslavement too threw strangers into the midst of a people's life. Such aliens might be of a much higher culture and were able, at any rate, to bring in new ideas. Their presence acted somewhat like that of the foreign wives. And the same is true of the trader; he might not be present long, but he was always the purveyor of news from the outside world.

Coming now to the exchange of material objects, we find that the trader is more than a news-carrier or a transporter of ideas. By bringing these material objects he introduces the actual instrumentalities of adjustment, as developed by one people, into the ken of another. Generally, in the early times, he was an agent of a higher culture to a lower; and so was able to bring to the latter a set of superior adjustments which might have taken centuries to develop in the regular way. In that sense he was a great educator and disseminator of civilization, without in the slightest degree, in the great majority of cases, intending to be.

The subject of trade has already been cited in other connections, but there are still some aspects of it to be developed. It is easily seen that if there were no division of labor, there would be no occasion for exchange, for all would have the same things, namely, the things which each had made for himself. But along with division of labor, or specialization, goes co-operation; and that implies exchange of commodities—unless, indeed, one set of men are slaves of another, when the movement of the product of labor is nearly all in one direction, the slaves giving all rather than participating in a fair exchange. The advantages of division of labor have been set forth in elementary treatises on economics; something needs to be said here about specialization by groups or peoples. For it is true that one group may be producing something very different from another. Some tribes have what is called a natural monopoly; they have a deposit of salt or flint, let us say, which neighboring groups envy. For a time a number of tribes fight for its possession, but after a while a better adjustment takes place and the tribes who do not possess the valuable deposit offer payment in goods of some kind for what salt or flint they need.

Most countries can produce some things better than they can others, and the easiest way to live is to specialize upon those products and to trade for what is more difficult or costly to produce. This is only common sense; but it is hard sometimes for people to act sensibly, especially if they live under a constant suspicion that their neighbors may presently, through hostility or for some other reason, refuse to trade with them any longer. Then they wish to be self-sufficient and to produce everything for themselves—a course that they would deem foolish in any individual.

In any case, many savage tribes have adopted the custom of specializing and of exchanging products; and it is plain enough that they have therein hit upon a superior adjustment in living. They have generally been willing, also, to exchange with a civilized people which, of course, can offer products which natives cannot make. The civilized trader has, let us say, guns or whiskey, for which the natives exchange ivory or furs. Each party is eager to exchange, for neither can produce what the other has to offer.

As it develops, exchange works out a certain mechanism of its own which is a high type of adjustment. When goods are traded for goods, that is known as swapping, or barter. But the inconvenience and confusion connected with trading things of unequal value led men to estimate values in terms of some well-known and common commodity, which thus became a standard of value. Beaver-skins were the standard in New England of the early colonial period, and tobacco in Virginia. Cattle, salt, beans, and many other commodities have been used as standards in different regions; the word *fee* and the term *pecuniary,* both going back to the Latin *pecus* (cattle) — the German word being *Vieh* — recall the time when cattle were money. When coined money is rare, people still drop back on some common commodity, as the soldiers in the World War used cakes of soap and bars of chocolate. In the Middle Ages, when coins were rare, men were paid for services in land. Having no money with which to hire soldiers, or even messengers or cooks, they took what they had — land — and used it much as we use money today. It is evident that any such standard of value discharges part of the function of money.

But money is more than a mere standard of value; there is need also of a circulating medium. Cows or land cannot pass from pocket to pocket. There are often small differences to allow for in a trade, as where one man swaps his horse for another and ten dollars " to boot." A more readily divisible money is needed; and swift on the need runs the adjustment. The Virginia tobacco was in pretty large bundles, and the New England beaver-skins could not be cut in pieces to " make change " without losing value. Hence the development of a circulating medium alongside the standard of value. This medium need not have much value in itself, any more than a poker-chip or a paper dollar; or it may have virtual face-value, like a gold eagle. If it has little value, it is sometimes called a " token." Such were the strings of discs used by the American Indians, called " wampum " — discs of shell, the dark ones being sometimes twice the value of the white, that is, worth twice as much in beaver-skins. Wampum had some intrinsic value; it cost some labor to make it, and it was used as ornament.

Money is one of the most clever adjustments ever made by man; it has had a further evolution into checks, drafts, and other modern devices; but its value always rests in the possibility of exchanging it for actual goods. Token-money is just as good as the credit of the party whose promise to redeem it at full face-value appears on its surface — just as good as the prospect of getting actual goods for the token when it is turned in. It is one of the functions of economics to analyze the vast mechanism of exchange which has evolved in recent centuries among the civilized nations. That mechanism is now too complicated for any but experts to understand; but it has all grown up by incessant and generally slight modifications of what went before, that is, by gradual adjustment through variation, selection, and transmission.

Along with the consideration of money as a mechanism of exchange should go that of weights and measures, which are likewise indispensable accessories to trade. Where money is a mere commodity, like gold-dust, or where it is not well standardized, it has to be measured or weighed like anything else, and cannot be accepted by count or tale. Thus Shylock carries a pair of scales about with him. We may begin with measures. A good many of them carry in their names the clue to the origin of them all, namely, in the ordinary rough estimates " by rule of thumb." We measure length by the " foot " or by stepping it off; thus the mile is a thousand paces (*mille passuum*). Horses are so many " hands " or " palms " (now four inches) in height; a charge for a musket, or for a glass of spirits, used to be so many " fingers " (twenty-four to the foot, or equivalent to four barley-corns, according to an arithmetic of 1600); the " span " of the hand (nine inches, in England), the reach of the outstretched arms (fathom, or six feet), the cubit or ell (length of the forearm, elbow to hand; variously estimated, but in the general neighborhood of a yard) : these are examples of the rough-and-ready methods of measurement upon which our own are based. We have adjusted and standardized, but have not utterly renounced those old prototypes. Similarly with the weights, though the names are not so significant. Still, the carat is the seed of a tree, a light counterpoise adapted to the weighing of great value in small bulk; and we still speak of " grains."

In contrast to such sets of adjustments, arrived at casually, and only gradually criticized and standardized, consider the metric system, which was carefully planned out ahead, and based upon a fundamental figure which was meant to be invariable. This figure was a ten-millionth of the distance from the pole to the equator; and the various measures of surface and capacity, and the several weights, were all brought into relation to this basic figure. But then the calculation of that basic distance was proved to be inexact, so that the meter is now an arbitrary measure of the old sort. It is worth remarking here that man gets nothing absolute on this earth. He gets approximations and variable standards. To what can a yardstick be compared, to see whether it is " right "? To another yardstick? Suppose even that there is a standard steel yardstick somewhere; it is nevertheless longer in heat than in cold. Of course it is possible to define the yard as the length of that steel rod at, say, sixty-five degrees Fahrenheit; but suppose — a thing not beyond imagination — that the rod were lost or destroyed; what then would a yard be?

Hitherto it has been rather assumed that buyer and seller, together with their goods, are close together. But both the goods and the persons must generally have come from some distance; and if the goods are quite different in character, like wool and pepper, which are the products of different zones, they have probably come from a considerable distance. In any case, trade would not get very far but for the development of *transportation*. To get any complete idea of exchanges, we must review, in some of its main aspects, the development of transportation. Routes and roads, both by land and sea, constitute an instructive set of adjustments to life-conditions; here we shall attend rather to the devices for carrying.

The first carrier was a human being, probably a woman; for in the division of labor practised between the sexes the man had to be unhampered for hunting, and the woman became a sort of draught-animal. In any case there were no vehicles or domestic animals, or even carrying-devices. One of the first of the latter to be developed is a basket or bag, carried on the back, with a strap to go over the forehead. Then came the pole, with the burden swung at the middle, and borne by two persons. Other such adjustments have been put to use by backward peoples, but they did not go very far. Land-transportation did not amount to much until after the domestication of animals. If human beings are the pack-animals, they have to be used in considerable numbers. Roosevelt took two hundred porters on his expedition.

The part played by the white-topped ox wagon in the history of South Africa and by the camel caravan in North Africa, has been played in middle Africa by the files of strong, patient, childlike savages, who have borne the burdens of so many masters and employers hither and thither, through and across, the dark heart of the continent. — Roosevelt, "African Game Trails," p. 23.

With the domestication of animals the efficiency of transportation, not of goods alone, but also of men, was greatly heightened. Pack-saddles and similar devices were constructed. One of the most primitive vehicles consisted of two poles suspended one on each side of a horse or dog, with the ends connected and dragging. The load rested across the poles, behind the animal. Later on, carts with wide wheels formed of a cross-section of a tree were evolved and gradually, by an improvement here and another there, the vehicle, and also the harness, approached their modern forms. One of the crucial discoveries in land-transportation was that of the wheel — which doubtless came from the primitive roller, employed in moving weights — the use of which obviated much of the friction encountered in dragging. Where the surface was of ice and snow, the sledge, with bone runners, remained the better adjustment — even the bone of the runners being superior, in the intense cold, to the more brittle iron or steel. Water was sometimes dropped upon the runners, there to freeze into a sheath. And while speaking of adjustments in transportation over snow, it is in place to mention the clever snow-shoes made by the Indians and the wooden snow-spectacles, with a thin slit to look through, which afforded protection against the glare on the snow, and consequent snow-blindness.

Water transportation has the advantage of much less friction and generally of greater smoothness. Rafts are among the crudest devices for traversing water; and, in some localities, basket-like craft or rather shapeless coracles of skin are employed, where the idea is simply to float on a river current, with a little steering. But most peoples who have taken to the water have developed boats with some shapeliness to them, capable of being directed and of being propelled by the men in them, even against wind and current. The dug-out or bark canoe is capable of carrying considerable loads, and so is the Eskimo skin-covered woman's-boat, or freight-boat. Such craft, propelled by paddles or oars, developed in size until the galley was evolved.

The Eskimo and Indians made little use of wind-power for transportation. This is one of the forces appropriated out of nature which might have been taken up along with fire and falling water; but since it was employed by savages virtually for sailing alone — not for wind-mills till a later period of culture — it has been left until now. As a matter of fact, the use of sails in any systematic manner is a comparatively late development. However, the Pacific Islanders sailed their canoes, which consisted of the canoe proper with an outrigger and often a sort of platform between, far and wide over the ocean. The general practice in primitive sailing is to let down the sheet and row when the wind is ahead; for the development of keel or centerboard, and the art of tacking, are achievements beyond most savages. Adjustments in the lines, rigging, and size of sailing-craft bring us finally to the clippers of the last century; then the steamer comes in and sailing-craft fall back in the competition.

Air transportation is even now in its infancy; it is mentioned merely to call attention to the adjustments man has had to make in trying to traverse a new and strange medium. Perhaps the time will come when the air-ship will cause the retirement of the water-vehicle, as the steam-engine threatens some time to render obsolete, even in the wide arid stretches, the " ship of the desert."

Beside its mechanisms of several sorts, trade has also its peculiar methods of adjustment to human desires. In a preceding lesson we have seen how human emotions can be evoked, with a resulting display of power in action, by the assurance of freedom and by appeals to patriotism or vanity. Trade also has its methods of appeal to wants; and shows devices capable of stirring latent wants, or even of creating wants. Such methods are, broadly, those of *suggestion,* or, to use a commoner term, of advertising.

What the trader is looking for, above all, is a demand for his goods; he himself will take care of the supply. He therefore caters to his customers' taste, supplying the savage with glass beads, brass wire, and trinkets; and, in general, adjusting his offerings to the stage of culture of his prospective customers. The Phœnicians of old were expert in this line; frontier-traders in general have followed it. Display of goods in what might be called an embryo market occurred in " silent barter " and at the trading-posts. There were displayed such articles as the natives wanted, or, according to the traders' experience, could be led to want. The tendency was, evidently, to suggest to the native the desirability of products that had not at first appealed to him. This is a lucrative process and also a civilizing one — but the trader's eye was on the former aspect only; the latter effect was incidental and accidental.

Stimulation of a demand for new commodities is a phenomenon of trade between peoples unequally advanced in culture; for one party must be offering new and unheard-of articles, and among neighboring savage peoples one tribe is not likely to be much ahead of the rest. In later times it is a method of setting afloat new variations — small differences — rather than a presentation of utter novelties; but it is almost indispensable for this purpose. It gives the new variation its chance, and sometimes, when the skill of the advertiser in suggestion is at its peak, a chance all out of proportion to its claims.

Finally, the successful trader is alert not to push the matter of transmission of new ideas and products too hard or too fast. If he feels contempt for the taste of prospective customers, he does not allow that to interfere with giving them what their untutored hearts desire. If they want credit, he acquiesces, not demanding cash but raising his prices to cover delays and risks in collection. In all these ways he shows himself a skillful adjuster and consequently is able, unconsciously, or at least not purposefully, to discharge his historic function of culture-carrier.

CHAPTER VIII

WAR AND GOVERNMENT

The adjustment of groups of men to their life-conditions, hitherto considered, have been chiefly adaptations to the physical environment; they have looked to greater success in the food-quest, to the utilization of materials and forces out of nature, and to the exchange of the results attained. But all through the preceding lessons there has appeared also a second type of environment, consisting of other groups of men — what might be called the *social environment*. Trade and transportation, as well as all other forms of coöperation and communication, require the presence of other societies. So that, although the emphasis hitherto has been given to adjustments to the natural or physical environment, it has been impossible to confine attention to those alone. But from now on the emphasis changes, and will rest upon adjustment to the social environment — though in these cases we shall be as little able to exclude the influence of physical nature as we have been, up to this point, in shutting out reference to relations with other tribes and nations. Classify as we will, the divisions we make are artificial, and run together in any picturing of actual life.

In the present lesson we are to seek the sense of that regulation which men put on themselves, and which we call government. The best approach to that subject is through consideration of war, and with that we shall begin.

There is a popular misconception about the savage, derived, no doubt, from vivid and horrifying accounts of certain tribes, which represents him as almost constantly at war. The facts do not support this view; savages quarrel a good deal, but "war " is a pretty large word for their bickerings and petty raidings for property and women. However, there are a good many fights on the small scale; and with the increase of population and of civilization the scale is increased, even though the frequency may be diminished.

The weapons of war are at first those of the chase; indeed, it would be hard in many cases, to distinguish warfare and hunting, for the former is often no more than a man-hunt, and the human quarry is not infrequently devoured after it is killed. In any case we have already gone sufficiently into the matter of weapons as adjustments, and shall consider warfare from the standpoint of the tactics and so-called "rules of war" developed in the early course of its evolution.

The warfare of savages is typically unsystematic and of but feeble organization. They fight, for the most part, singly and without much coöperation. It has always been difficult to get them to adopt European tactics and to fight in bodies, and they have been used most successfully as irregulars, and particularly as scouts. The Indians picked out each his tree or rock and fought what often amounted to a series of duels. Every warrior was about like every other one; the only specialization between man and man lay between the chief and others. Yet the chief plunged into the fray with the rest, and did not remain behind the line — perhaps several miles behind — as in modern warfare. The only commissary department was the women, who brought up food to the fighters. They sometimes carried the extra arms and lent aid to the wounded. Lack of food-provision explains why backward peoples have seldom been able to prosecute a close or long siege; for they have had to turn aside to raid for supplies, as they did about the city of Troy, or in the attack on the castles of the feudal age.

This amounts to saying that their adjustments allowing of the successful prosecution of war were but slightly developed. They took a good deal of their fighting out in boasting and threatening, in sound and fury of the voice; generally the fighting itself was sharp and brief, and did not go to a finish. The worsted party hauled off for repairs and the victors turned to the enjoyment of the spoils and to the celebration of their own magnificence. Male captives were either adopted or put to death, though women and children might be simply appropriated; later on, both males and females were enslaved. There was not much idea of acquiring territory as such; there were raids and then a retirement, with the booty, back home. Another tribe might be held tributary, but there was seldom anything like expansion or empire-building. Consider the " empire " of Attila and the Huns. A migratory people might take up a new location, killing and driving out the natives, or even enslaving them; but it took people of a higher culture to make and consolidate conquests.

At first there were no rules of warfare, but fighting men was like hunting animals — any expedient that produced the result would do. There was no idea of a " fair fight " any more than there is now in a conflict between a man and a snake. To plant thorns tipped with poison in the path over which barefooted enemies were accustomed to pass was an admirable expedient. It was all right to make an unprovoked attack, unannounced by declaration of hostilities; to assail from the rear or from ambush; to poison the enemy's water-supply; or to do any thing else whatsoever that might get results. To match some of these barbaric performances it is necessary to come clear up to modern times, with their poison gases, distribution of disease-germs among cattle and men, maltreatment of prisoners and of non-combatants, and other practices introduced by modern barbarians.

But, as time went on, a number of savage tribes developed what might be called the germs of chivalry. They gave prisoners at least a theoretic chance for life in running the gantlet; they declared war before beginning it; they banished poisoned weapons; allowed truces and guaranteed the safety of emissaries; spared the women and children; and otherwise adhered to rules of conduct in warfare. This was a series of adjustments which rendered war less destructive and left the combatants, after the fight, less incensed at each other and less averse to the resumption of peaceful relations. There are some people in this country who are incapable for life of friendly feeling toward Germany, but who cherish no great resentment toward those of her allies who were not so ready to adopt any means whatsoever to win, regardless of the customary rules of war.

Warfare may be said to be one of the functions of the state; but we have treated it first because it is a good starting-point from which to approach the whole topic of government. For the final test of the stability of all forms of early government was war; and all those forms, and most of the later ones, reveal a sort of family resemblance to the military organization. Where tribes have no warfare, as was virtually the case with the Eskimo, they have no governmental organization; and it is in the militant state that government becomes most thorough-going and oppressive. In time of war powers are lodged in the government which it could not attain in time of peace. Court-martial may take the place of civil courts. *Inter arma silent leges* — amidst arms laws hold their peace. We have elected a number of military heroes president, and elevation to that office has never been hindered by the possession of a military record. The glamor of the uniform and of military exploits has never ceased to impress humanity, and to the leader in war have often been ascribed civic virtues which he may not have possessed at all. These facts establish the close relation between war and government, which will be repeatedly revealed as we go on.

Roughly it might be said that the function of government is to afford *security* from outside forces and *order* among those within. The former cannot be attained in the absence of the latter; so we might begin with the internal function. In their relations with one another, members of the same community follow a code of customary behavior, which limits the freedom of each in the interest of the whole. If no one is free to murder or to steal at will, then everyone has a right to life and to property. If people are restrained from crossing a city street as if it were a country road, then too is the traffic suspended now and then to let them cross without danger. All parties are robbed of freedom in one form while they are being assured of it in another. The result of this is orderliness; and whether or not " order is heaven's first law," it is the basic need in a society. These customary actions, many of which are mere conventions and not laws at all, such as thanking even a stranger for a small service, are the rules of the game of living in a society — rules without which social life would be a sordid and disorderly scramble, punctuated by shovings and pushings, disputes, cursings, rough-and-tumble encounters, bloodshed, and deaths.

Such rules or conventions, gradually evolved in the process of living, represent the ultimate basis of a society's adjustment to its life-conditions. Customs of this sort surround all the interests of life, prescribing behavior in all cases, from gait and posture to forms of marriage and the family and of religious exercises. Some of them are trivial, and do not last long, for example, styles; others are to be found at nearly all times and places, as, for instance, rules conferring superior rights upon men as compared with women. The most important of these customary regulations are at length set down in the form of *laws*. It is evident that a lawless tribe, whose members are always disorderly and distracted by quarrels and uproars, can stand no chance in a competition with an orderly one. If it comes to war, the former will go under; and if there is an industrial or commercial rivalry, it will be set back and impoverished. *Law and order* are a society's absolutely indispensable adjustments for living at all, or living well.

Now the force behind all these rules of conduct in social

life, of whatever kind, provided they are not to be dead letter, is *public opinion*. Public opinion, however, generally requires some agency to carry out its judgments. In minor matters it does its own expressing, and through such means as ostracism and ridicule suppresses types of behavior that are unconventional and not according to custom. But, by reason of the fact that " what is everybody's business is nobody's business," the enforcement of the rules of conduct would be partial, intermittent, and spotty, were it not for the development of an executive instrumentality. This is the chief or king, to whom, as Homer says, the deity has entrusted the scepter and the customary precedents. He is to enforce the rules, and that means that he is to pass on cases of alleged transgression; hence the chief is both judge and executive. His law-making function is relatively unimportant. He never really gets the power to make lasting laws, for public opinion, even under a despot, will at length upset him if he defies it flatly enough.

The chief is likely to be a product of war. No tribe except those that live in extreme isolation is safe from its neighbors. Suppose, now, that a tribe which has attended pretty well to internal orderliness gets into war with another. Its very existence is threatened; and if it is not to go under, it hits upon the expedient of intrusting its fate to a strong individual. It is said that no war was ever won by a debating-society. Unity of command was forced even upon the Allied Nations, as a necessary condition for the winning of the World War. Power and responsibility go together, and in the warring tribes some promising man — say a mighty hunter — is endowed with power and then held responsible. One after another commander may fail, as in the Civil War — the result being a more or less protracted selection which ultimately brings out the capable chief. Then, whatever may have been the system of appointing chiefs in time of peace — whether upon the basis of old age and wisdom in the matter of the customs and precedents, or upon the basis of heredity, or without reference to sex — the war-chief is likely to retain his power and to displace the peace-chief. This is especially the case if a number of wars follow one another, without much interval between them. In so far war is a chief-maker. And, whether or not the peace-chief becomes the war-chief, the powers of the executive are sure to be greatly increased; further, since power is not readily laid down, Cincinnatus-fashion, war strengthens the chieftainship, where it does not create it.

For all practical purposes, if we wish to trace the evolution of government, we may begin with the adjustment known as an unlimited monarchy. It is never totally unlimited, for the basic element of all is public opinion; and even the absolute ruler may not safely go counter to it. It is interesting to note that the war-chiefs of certain Indian tribes could be dismissed and reduced to the ranks by the matrons. In truth, as time goes on there is a constant subtraction from the power of the despot; and the parts subtracted are distributed among other agencies. This means that public opinion senses the fact that, except at a pinch, it is not well to leave all the power in one hand. There exist, then, councils which the chief is obliged to consult and which may overrule his will; and, besides these councils, even on a quite undeveloped stage of civilization, there also appear assemblies of the whole tribe, to which the chief must present his plans for approval or disapproval. This was the situation among the Germans when they broke into the Roman Empire.

It might even be said that a people first makes a single expression of its public opinion by surrendering all its rights to an opinion; its opinion (which is not thought out, but is simply based upon experience) is that it shall have no opinion outside of the chief's. He is to decide for everyone, so long as he does not antagonize the interests of too many people. But it would seem that, later on, society repented of signing away its power of self-expression, and began (again without anyone thinking the whole matter out) to take back its delegated powers by evolving various expedients for *representation*. The councils and assemblies see to it that somebody beside the executive shall have a chance to have a say as to the tribal policy. This process goes on until the executive holds his position only by keeping an " ear to the ground "; by seeking to forecast public opinion and to anticipate or fall in with it. The whole process might be called the progressive freeing or enfranchisement of public opinion.

Nevertheless, however free that opinion becomes, it always needs agencies for its expression. It needs to be organized in order to make itself felt; and thus arise parties of one kind and another. All who hold the same views, or, to put it more exactly, all whose interests lead them to hold the same views, get together and support one another. They raise a rhythmic clamor that brings pressure to bear on those who hold power and who wish to continue to hold it. The latter adjust, if they are wise, to the expressions of the powerful parties; though sometimes they can bring the masses of the people to support them by showing the objectors that their real interests are going to be served by so doing. This is the educational function of the true statesman. Demagogues are " leaders of the people " (that is what the word means) who cajole them, or impress them by dramatic actions and talk, or skillfully divert their attention from the main issue. They may, for a time, lead the masses, by playing upon their emotions, to favor the retention or even the introduction of what will be a maladjustment; but, in the long run, the real interests of the people make themselves unmistakably felt, and then no maladjustment can last. For a maladjustment in the field ends by irritating those whose interests are thwarted, even though they do not know what is the matter; and then they start a revolution, or vote the government out of office, and the new government starts afresh. Since it gets in by criticizing what went before, it is more than likely to reverse (or pretend to reverse) former policies, good as well as bad — but along with the good, also the bad. If it does not relieve the soreness, it too is rejected, and some one of its successors does the proper adjusting. This is a groping, hit-or-miss procedure; of course, as people develop in experience and understanding, an opposition party is more likely to recognize and expose a maladjustment by a direct attack.

In the course of time the executive is stripped of his once almost universal power, and we have the division of government into the legislative, executive, and judicial branches. But these branches cannot be kept forever apart. If war comes, the executive regains power, and sometimes, even in highly civilized countries, enjoys a practical dictatorship, such as President Wilson held for part of his term. Again, judges can make new law, or legislate, by their interpretation of existing statutes; they represent a delicate agency of adjustment whose operations may not be perceived as are those of the legislative bodies. And legislatures may hamper the executive so severely as to be themselves, in some sense, the executive power. Such classification of governmental agencies, like any other classification, is not hard and fast; but its categories run into one another and blur.

Further, any one of these main agencies in government has to be subdivided. A President of the United States cannot do all the executive work of the country, particularly if he has to do the law-making too, as he sometimes has to when Congress does not live up to its responsibilities. And so there are governors, mayors, and a multitude of other executives. Local legislative bodies pass state laws and city ordinances; and courts run all the way from a Supreme Court to police-courts. As we go back in history, these subdivisions run back into the division from which they have branched, as the twigs run back into larger branches, until, at length, all recede into the trunk of government, namely, the chief. All receive their support and sustenance from public opinion, which, in our analogy, would be represented by the mother-earth out of which the tree springs. Public opinion is formed upon interests and gets its driving power from the emotions that attend interests as they are seen — or, more properly, as they are sensed or felt. The whole governmental structure is a set of adjustments for the realization of interests; and the basic interests of society are subserved by whatever secures for it that law and order without which the society could not endure.

A society within which law and order rule is sometimes called a *peace-group.* The name explains itself. Every family must be a peace-group to persist. Then there is a group composed of a number of families, say, a tribe; and it too must be a peace-group. A number of tribes may form a larger body, say, a nation; and several nations, such as the Six Nations, may form a confederacy, such as the League of the Iroquois Indians. As these groups join they merge their government and laws into a larger and more comprehensive whole. They may keep certain parts of their local government, but these may not be inconsistent with the general government. It is always a question as to how far uniting states are willing to give up their local freedom in favor of central control. There are advantages in both, and there are often hitches between what we Americans call " state rights " and the " federal government." These hitches are the more serious and threaten unification most — or even render it well-nigh impossible — when sections that are united, or might unite, have different sets of adjustments to radically different life-conditions. The South had a warmer climate and, largely because of that, a social life differing widely from that of the North. The outstanding difference was slavery. Of a consequence the American Union was threatened when the two sections came into collision. The Union could not exist " half slave and half free." The suppression of this salient point of difference, along with a number of others allied to it, resulting in the Northernizing of the South, allowed the Union to go on. In the case of the Carolingian Empire, where there was a conflict between the local authorities and the central government, the former won; and the Empire split into a multitude of petty states.

The reader has noticed that the process of unification, or of enlargement of the peace-group, stops with the nation. If he asks himself why this enlargement may not proceed, let him note the difference between nations in their forms of social adjustment, that is, in the type of their civilization. Not alone are the uncivilized nations in great contrast with the civilized, or even the half-civilized, but there are striking differences between the different highly civilized countries themselves. Language is one of the most deep-seated of these, and one of the most difficult to overcome; religion is another; and these are but two out of thousands of divergences. Recognition of these differences has always caused a nation to think well of itself and poorly of others; there is a certain national egotism which leads nations to look down on all others and to ridicule their language, habits, and institutions. The ground does not look favorable to an extension of the peace-group, so that it may be actually international. Nations have not been able, apparently, to get together, as the constituent parts of nations have done.

And yet there are propositions leading to unification, and their chief object is to attain peace and order between nations. These proposals fix their attention on the likenesses, not the differences; and also on the removal or reconciliation of differences. All the civilized nations are essentially similar in their material adjustments, that is, in their economic life, and not so dissimilar in their forms of property, of marriage and the family, and even of government. As for their industry and trade, in those, whether they will or not, they must stand or fall together. And the last great war has demonstrated to most thinking men, and to many who do not think but only feel, that whatever else nations do, they cannot afford to have another world-conflict. " Never again! " was the soldiers' watch-word; but it is also that of any person endowed with even the germs of reason. Every nation which went into the late war, including the aggressors, had an excuse ready; and not over one of two of them, even in the secrecy of their own minds, believed war to be a good thing. The world wanted, and now wants still more, some substitute adjustment in place of war. That is undoubtedly the verdict of international public opinion. Well, the only substitute is peace; and the burning question now is how to get and assure it.

And the only hint from experience is that given by the evolution of the smaller, national peace-group. The fact is that for centuries nations have been gradually establishing a set of customs and agencies making for peace between nations. These are, of course, adjustments of the several nations to their life-conditions, or environment; for the environment of any nation is formed, in good part, by other nations. Such adjustments are treaties, alliances, diplomatic agencies, postal unions, to say nothing of endless trading-agreements, concessions, consulates, and other agencies that promote coöperation instead of hostility. No one ever expects to see a super-state, ruling all mankind; but a world-judiciary seems to be thought feasible by many experts, and the possibility of an international law that shall cover relations between nations has been in the air for centuries, and has been partly realized in practice, like customary law, though it may not have been codified. All civilized nations united to condemn and punish piracy and slavery, and there are certain other afflictions that affect all nations and which cannot well be suppressed except by joint action; for instance, the white-slave traffic, or various diseases.

Because the proposed agencies are faulty is no reason for doing nothing except to await the next world-war and the crippling of civilization and human well-being for an indefinite future. The interests of all nations are now pretty much the same. Five centuries ago it mattered no whit to Manhattan Island what was happening in what is now Servia; but in

1914 it mattered a great deal to New York. By reason of man's extension of connections, Timbuctoo is now nearer to Boston than New York was awhile ago. Evade the issue as we will, the fact is that our life-conditions now include all nations, and that we must, if we would not suffer, but live, and live better, adjust to the situation that has developed. What that adjustment will be is a matter of prediction and so does not fall within our range of treatment. But law and order, the basic results of government, will be somehow extended beyond national boundaries: public opinion against war will have its way; the peace-group will be broadened — or the penalty of maladjustment will be paid.

CHAPTER IX

MARRIAGE AND THE FAMILY

The preceding chapters have treated of adjustments which have enabled societies to live, or to live better, in the face of natural conditions and in the presence of other men. We come now to another set of adjustments peculiar to human beings, which are evoked in response to the fact that the race consists of two sexes. The presence of sex has called for adjustments that take account of the essential differences between man and woman, and also of the presence of children. Sex is one of those life-conditions which, like gravitation or climate, must be accepted as they are; it is adjusted to by certain arrangements which, in their developed, institutional form, we know as marriage and the family.

If societies did not practice various devices for securing a food-supply, for defending themselves, and for keeping order, they could not last except upon some low and beast-like plane of life. And if they did not adjust themselves to the condition of sex — in particular if they did not somehow bring it about that offspring should be protected and reared — society could not last beyond one generation. For mankind cannot now leave these matters to instinct, and never has been able to do so, so far as any direct evidence possessed by us, even concerning backward tribes, is able to reveal.

So far as providing for the continuance of the species is concerned, the plants and the lower animals depend chiefly upon producing so many seeds or eggs that, despite a heavy destruction, enough will still survive to carry on the stock. The female fish, for example, simply lays thousands of eggs and goes off, paying no further attention to them. Farther up the scale of being, however, fewer young are produced, and greater care and protection are afforded them. The hen takes care of the chicks for a time, and the cat of the kittens. Sometimes the male assists in this task. But in all cases, whatever is done is at the urge of instinct. Human mother-love is also instinctive, though among some of the lowest peoples it does not last long. It is only when father and mother unite in caring for the children that they receive that support and protection in infancy which are needful for the attainment of healthy maturity. That the parents shall be associated in that function, it is generally necessary that they shall live together in a relationship not existing in nature but demanded by social custom, namely, marriage.

We have considered the case of the children first because the rearing of the younger generation is a vital necessity to the endurance of human society; and the better the adjustment looking to their welfare, the stronger the society grows as time goes on. Numbers always count in any competition, and the society that can rear the most numerous and healthy offspring has the commanding advantage in the struggle. Though we can see this plainly enough, the savage, lacking in knowledge and perspective, could not figure it out; and so, in our search for the needs to which marriage formed the expedient adjustment, we must expect to discover something more fundamental than the desire to rear young.

What we discover from the examination of hundreds of instances is that primitive marriage is predominantly an economic alliance — a case of coöperation in the struggle for existence. Woman is physically weaker than man, and is otherwise unfitted for strenuous hunting or fighting. She is almost never found doing either; but what she does is just as important, for she keeps the fire and carries the household gear from camp to camp. She does, and apparently prefers to do, just what man does not want to do; and he likes to do what she is unable to do. Both functions, so absolutely necessary for well-being, cannot well be covered by the same person. Two men, or two women, seeking to apportion between them these two sets of tasks, would quarrel and rebel — just as a party of men who are camping out rebel at " kitchen police." The two sets of tasks are supplementary as well as necessary; and the adjustment whereby they are assigned to two persons who are by nature supplementary, represents an apt arrangement of living. In many important respects, even today, by reason of the supplementary nature of the sexes, a combination of man and woman is stronger than one of man and man, or woman and woman.

In the course of time, if not from the outset, man was able by reason of being the fighter, with the better weapons and the discipline, to force woman to the monotonous and uninteresting tasks, whether she was willing or not. Whether the arrangement was agreeable to her or not made no difference. Yet it is a great error to suppose that savage women are always ill treated and ever bemoaning their sad and oppressed lot. They are not; they live on into their destiny cheerfully, knowing no other and so taking it as a matter of course. It has become customary and is unquestioned. The traveler among the Indians reports the squaws always digging in the corn-field or doing other hard work, while the braves lie about and smoke. But the latter have often just got home from miles of wandering after game, and miles of heavy burden-bearing in bringing it home, things which the women could not have done; while the women have worked along at low pressure on their less strenuous tasks, feeling no resentment whatsoever as they viewed their lords and masters lolling about the camp, and raising no questions as to the " fairness " of the arrangement.

The study of simple societies shows us that there is work which is, by long-established custom, woman's, and other work which is man's; but that, whatever the details of this arrangement, it represents a typical instance of that effective expedient which we have learned to know as division of labor (or specialization of function) accompanied by coöperation. When the sexes specialize, their coöperation is in the form of marriage, just as when groups specialize, theirs is in that of trade. Although one may think that woman gets less out of this combination than man, yet she is held to it by an added interest, namely, the powerful instinct of maternal love. Men do not show anything similar. So the woman with a child needs the help of a man, inasmuch as it is practically impossible, under savage conditions, for a mother to carry on the struggle for existence, unaided, for herself and child.

In any case we find marriage in some form practised by all, or nearly all, known peoples. Men have quarreled, all through history, over property and women; and it was for the welfare of society that a woman should be somehow assigned to some particular man, and that man's right to her person and labor firmly guaranteed by custom and by law. This was one of the ways of securing the peace and order which are so necessary to the welfare of any society. And when there was property to inherit, it was of the utmost importance to know just what persons in the next generation were to get it. The heirs were the legitimate children, that is to say, the children of the woman who had been married to the deceased owner of the property in the way recognized by the tribe as customary and proper. This prevented disputes over the other great cause of quarreling, namely, property. Thus marriage was an expedient which helped everybody concerned into a better adjustment for living. It reconciled the various parties to it — not only the two principal parties, but parents and children, relatives, and fellow-tribesmen of all degrees of nearness. It is one of the basic adjustments achieved by society — a great institution working in customary responses to vital needs.

Within the general institution of marriage developed the organization known as the family. This was a combination of all who were related, or were supposed to be related, by blood, also generally including the women who had married male members and sometimes the men who had married female members. In some cases it covered also the slaves—called *famuli* by the Romans, as constituting part of the *familia*. The family was an organization which further harmonized the interests of all members, generally under the authority of a patriarch, or father-ruler, and amounted to a sort of miniature government, with all the virtues of such in keeping order and peace. In fact, the family was one of the first peace-groups. Within it the children were reared and disciplined. It is clear that a strong family constituted an excellent arrangement for the raising to maturity of the next generation; and, though it cannot be said that either marriage or the family rose exclusively for the sake of the children, yet the latter came, in time, to be the chief interest of the family, and, on the whole, those benefiting most from its existence.

It seems that the race has wrestled with this need of adjustment to the fact of sex, more or less gropingly, from the most primitive stages. Every thinkable arrangement has been tried: polygyny, where a man had several wives; polyandry, where a woman had several husbands; monogamy, where one husband had one wife at a time; and what is called pair-marriage, where a single pair held together until one or the other died. In most primitive cases the wife was bought, and was proud of it and of the price she brought to her father; again, she brought a dowry, and plumed herself upon its size — this being, in a sense, husband-buying. Sometimes there were mutual gifts. In some cases the girl had no choice, but was handed over by her father to whomsoever he wished; but in most instances she could have her way — she could elope, for example, with the man of her choice, and if they were not caught promptly, the marriage stood.

It was not permitted for any man to marry any woman; for

there were many prohibitions in restraint of unions. The oldest seems to be that which forbids the marriage of near kin. The union of a brother and a sister has been regarded by most human societies with horror; and some tribes do not allow persons of the same totem—that is, with the same legendary animal-ancestor—to marry. Among the Indians a Turtle may not marry a Turtle, but must "cross the totem," that is, marry a Hawk or a Bear. It is not to be thought that savages knew of the asserted ills of close inbreeding, for they regularly permitted certain persons to marry while absolutely prohibiting others, though all parties might be cousins and so be equally closely related. Some peoples required marriage within certain small groups and some insisted upon marriage outside. It can be shown that a small group will get on better by not restricting its unions to its own members; we have seen the advantages of intermarriage along with those of trade and other arrangements that promote exchange of culture (ch. VII, above). Of a consequence, it is not at all surprising to find out-marriage (exogamy) adopted by primitive progressives, while in-marriage (endogamy) lasts on only among tribes that are backward.

There has always existed, however, a prejudice against unions outside of one's class, or religion, or color. There is some sense in this, for if people of very different manner of life or belief marry, the difficulty of living in harmony is likely to be much increased, the marriage is less likely to be a fortunate one, and its bad consequences, both for the participants and for society, brand it as a poor adjustment. Any union between beings so different in every way as the sexes is likely to require a good deal of adjustment, and to start out with extra differences is to make the adjustment the more difficult. But some of the prohibitions have no sense at all; for instance, the one which, for a long time, forbade a man to marry his deceased wife's sister—the precise person whom he might best marry, in the majority of cases, if he wants to. Only within the last generation has this prohibition been repealed in England.

That marriage is, even to savage eyes, a very important thing to do aright, is witnessed by the multitude of prohibitions, both sensible and senseless, which have been put into force around the world. Savages know nothing about adjustment, but experience has taught them where one is needed and they take no chances about insisting upon marrying in the right and proper way, as it seems to them. No sentimental considerations are allowed to interfere and a union contrary to custom is severely and often savagely punished.

The important feature of a real marriage was the wedding ceremony. There was once little courting, and the proposal was generally made to the girl's father, often by the father of the suitor; but it was of the utmost importance to have everyone know who had married whom. For the fact that a certain woman belonged to a certain man, and that her children had a right to his property, was something to be published far and wide in the interests of peace and order. It was publicity that was sought in the wedding ceremony. There was no other way to get publicity except by a ceremony, and there were no other records save the recollections of living witnesses. Hence the elaborate and lavish set of rites and feastings that accompanied entrance into the status of matrimony. They look like mere ostentation, gorging, and drunkenness; but they have performed, through the ages, an important social function. Many another savage ceremony appears equally extravagant and meaningless until its true service as an adjustment amidst local life-conditions is appreciated.

It is interesting to notice that the wedding ceremony is often a sort of rehearsal of the future duties of man and wife. The man must bring in game, or otherwise show his capacity as provider; and the woman must cook some food or even dig a plot of garden. The man must strike the woman or otherwise indicate who is to be who in the new relation. The woman may take a child on her lap, to foreshadow her hoped-for motherhood. The garments of the two may be tied together. And if the wedding shows what wedlock is to be, divorce shows what it ought to have been and was not; it shows, in particular, what was expected of the wife. For the chief reasons for divorce are infidelity, inefficiency as a worker, and barrenness, this proving that a wife's chief duty is to be faithful, industrious, and fruitful.

It has been intimated that marriage was not, in its simplest forms, for the sake of children; but that element entered as the institution evolved. Children were wanted chiefly for the sake of support in old age, of keeping up the family, and of security in the future life. The first two of these reasons explain themselves, but it is necessary to give an added word to the third. Many peoples believe that unless one leaves children when he dies, he cannot get on at all in the next life, for he will have nobody to sacrifice food and other necessities to him. Thus he will have no support, and will have to leave the spirit-world; and not only that, but, as some believe, all his forefathers will be expelled along with him. This idea calls for an adjustment to what most civilized peoples would consider an imaginary or fanciful condition; but it is very real to those who hold such a belief. Consequently it is widely customary to adopt children if one has had none of his own or has lost them. Such notions evidently lead their holders to see in children the chief reason for marriage; and it is easy for them to read their own ideas into the savage's mind instead of trying to see just what was actually in that mind. One must give up judging other people by himself if he is to understand the truth of such matters.

Allusion has been made in a foregoing paragraph to plural marriage. In a general way, the number of wives a man had depended upon his wealth, so that even in a polygamous country the poorer people are likely to be monogamous. Wives were really an investment. We are told how the negro of south-central Africa will go down to the mines and work until he has accumulated some savings, which he invests in cattle. Having driven these home, he uses most of them in purchasing wives and then settles down to comfort for the rest of his days, while they support him. If they are lazy he feels much aggrieved; and such a disappointed investor has been known to appeal to the missionaries, asking them to persuade his wives to do their duty. Naturally, in regions where such a set of customs prevails, a man is glad to have many daughters, for their sale into wedlock makes him rich.

However, the adjustment represented by plural marriage has tended to pass away with the increase of civilization; and there are many reasons for believing that monogamy is a better arrangement for advanced peoples, whether the marrying parties are wealthy or not. The family is more closely bound together when there is but one father and one mother; inheritance is clearer and less complicated; there is less jealousy and dissension within the family; the children get better care for both their bodies and their characters; the affection between the spouses is likely to be stronger because it is concentrated between two persons and not diffused among many. Doubtless polygamy is an arrangement better calculated to increase brute numbers, and numbers were a great consideration on the earlier stages; but monogamy fosters quality rather than quantity of offspring; and quality rather than quantity is the desirable thing as civilization increases.

What is wanted in a wife, on the lower stages, is a rude sort of coöperation which is well enough in its way, and truly indispensable; but evolution, here as elsewhere, has refined these early relations into a much more delicate adjustment. The idea of the wife among the most advanced peoples is something as different from that out of which it has been refined as a hair-spring for a watch is different from the lumps of iron ore just taken from the mine. And yet the essential basis is the same, namely, coöperation. No marriage, savage or civilized, can be a success unless husband and wife pull together and are genuine help-mates. Once they coöperated in more material things alone, and they must continue to do that, for life is based upon the practical; but with the refinement, under evolution, of the marital relations, there comes about a partnership in things of the mind and spirit without which the material coöperation is insufficient.

To get a refined product there must always be something — and it is generally hard and coarse material — to refine. It is nothing against marriage that it began in crudity. Law was at first mere retaliation and religion mere ghost-fear. But you must have something with power and force in it to begin with, or there is nothing worth refining. You do not make a hair-spring out of clay, but out of something with strength and elasticity concealed within it, and capable of being brought out.

The early forms of family organization show force rather than delicacy. Man is the ruler over woman by virtue of his strength of body and of the fact that men have the weapons and discipline of the fighter and hunter. Often he does not hesitate to use his power in the most brutal manner. In many cases the father has the power of life and death over all members of the family, and is quite as despotic as the chief. Indeed, he is the chief of his family — the patriarch — and if the family is large, his position amounts to the headship of a considerable body of human beings. Here is where the family organization and that of the state run together. Compared with the male head of the family all other members seem to fall into nothingness. In particular the women seem to have no rights at all, but to be virtually property and slaves — property that can be sold at will and slaves to be worked up to their full capacity.

In such cases the position of woman seems, to the eye of the civilized observer, very low. As a matter of fact, however, women have always possessed considerable influence, and even where they are worked hard they are often consulted, with a most astonishing deference, as to tribal policy. Where they are able to hold their end up in the battle of life — where, for instance, they are the agriculturists who are able to contribute their part, along with the game taken by the hunters, to the joint welfare — they are usually highly valued and accorded much consideration. Savages are in the midst of the battle of life, with destruction always possible; and they cannot fail to recognize services that help to win the battle. The women can profit by this recognition, and do so profit, where their contribution to the food-supply or their other services plainly count in the struggle. Furthermore, they are almost always respected as mothers of children.

Later on, with the attainment of some security in the struggle for existence, life becomes less rough-and-ready, and there is a chance for the recognition of the less obvious and crude services of woman. Brute strength counts for less, and at length there develop sentiments of chivalry toward women, and a tendency to concede to them rights of whose existence no one dreamed, and the lack of which the women did not feel, during the strenuous period where everything had to be subordinated to mere living. The position of woman has really been determined by her status in the family, for it is to that status that all women among undeveloped peoples are destined; and so the rights and privileges of the unmarried or widowed go back to those of the wife as to a determining factor. The maiden is to be a wife; the widow has been one; and where they now are is either in preparation for wifehood or in continuation of it. For a time, and sometimes for her whole life, the widow remains so intimately associated with her deceased husband that no one dares to have anything to do with her, lest the ghost of the dead man be provoked.

It can be seen that the fact that the two sexes and the children must somehow get along with one another presented a great and complicated life-condition, and one altogether too difficult to be worked out by the savage's intellect. Even that of the civilized man has not been able to work it out to general satisfaction. But through experience adjustments were gradually made, to certain types of which we give such names as polygamy or monogamy; while to the whole combination of adjustments and organizations, including everything from proposal to divorce, we attach the term marriage. Marriage is the inclusive institution by which society automatically takes care of its own perpetuation.

CHAPTER X

RELIGION

We have considered the adjustment of men to the physical and to the social environments — to nature and to fellow-men — and at first sight it would appear that there is no further type of environment to which men are called upon to adapt. But upon studying the life of human society, one speedily discovers that a large part of men's attention has been monopolized by an environment of ghosts and spirits. Whether there is actually any such environment or not, men have been so sure of its existence that they have gone through all the motions of adjustment to it, and have developed masses of customs and a great institution in so doing. In a study of the development of the institutions of society we may not omit what is in some ways the most interesting and certainly not the least important, merely because it was evolved in response to life-conditions which may not be regarded as genuine.

To any thinking man the mysteries that surround life are evident enough; but most of us no longer cherish the views about them that men began with. Rather do we look down upon such notions as the savage holds about superhuman beings as childish and "superstitious." But we must recall the fact, already emphasized, that the beginnings of others of our most prized institutions, such as the family, were crude and unedifying. There is in the history of institutions a day of small things which one must not be too contemptuous of. Much more enlightening is it to look tolerantly into the simple notions of undeveloped men and try to see the reason for the holding of beliefs that seem to us indefensible. For it may be taken as a self-evident principle that human beings have not tried to make mistakes and deceive themselves. Living, especially for savages, is too serious a matter to be frivolous about. If people seem perverse and almost deliberately wrong-headed, it is not because they choose to be so; and if we look patiently into their circumstances, we generally find that, in their situation, we should probably not do any better than they. The trouble with primitive people is usually ignorance rather than evil intent; and it is not safe to assume that they are all idiots. Their minds are, as we have seen, pretty good; but there is not much in them. They lack knowledge.

Much happens to anyone which he cannot fully explain or even account for at all. If he is an ignorant person, he takes recourse to the wildest theories, for he has no power of criticism over any imaginings that occur or are suggested to him. What an ignorant person does not understand, he is likely to refer to magic. Even now, we call a man who does wonderful things that we do not understand, a " wizard." Applied to a man like Edison, the term is merely an exaggerated expression and is not meant seriously; but some of Edison's scientific predecessors, in the Middle Ages, were not only called wizards because they did things quite inexplicable at the time, though commonplace now, but they were persecuted and tortured, not at all playfully, as magicians and sorcerers. Ignorance has been inclined, throughout the race's history, to ascribe to supernatural power what it did not understand.

But the ignorance of today, or even of the mediæval period, is bright enlightenment compared with that of primitive man. His knowledge was a feeble and flickering candle-flame in a vast abyss of darkness. He knew what would happen if he applied fire to wood, and took it as a matter of course, needing no explanation; so, too, the rising of the sun took place every morning, and a man was a fool who wasted his time wondering about it. But a fiery bolt from the clouds that could shatter a tree and start a fire, or an eclipse of the sun, was an unusual happening that he could not account for as we now can. He knew nothing of electricity, nor of the possibility of the moon coming between the sun and the earth at regular, predictable periods. The realm of the inexplicable shut down upon him pretty close.

The fact is that the wisest man comes very shortly to the end of his knowledge and faces unexplainable mysteries; but he has already learned that many things that were impossible of explanation once are so no longer, and when he faces matters which he does not yet understand, like the nature of some subtle disease, he does not fly to a supernatural explanation but believes that many of those mysteries will be accounted for in time, and by natural law. He reserves supernatural power to account for things which he believes otherwise impossible of explanation. The savage has no such accumulation of recorded experience behind him, and so he must forthwith refer to spiritual agencies such common phenomena as evaporation, the winds, the reflections of a mirror, or the echo. The deeper his ignorance, the more things will he refer directly to supernatural agencies.

It is not that the savage goes about wondering and trying to explain things to himself because he has a natural curiosity. All the evidence shows that he is not curious along such lines. What brings the necessity of explanation home to him is the suffering of pain or fright in the presence of some happening which he does not know how to avoid or prevent in future. He is chronically afraid of bad luck, and rightly so; for his life is so insecure that he cannot afford to incur mischance. He is walking on the edge of existence, and cannot stand a push of even a few inches at the hand of ill luck; while if he were farther from the edge, as the civilized man is, he could submit to be jolted rather roughly without going over. When something novel occurs that does not hurt him or rouse his fear, he is indifferent. It takes a need and an interest to promote an effort in the direction of adjustment. That need is represented by apprehension lest that with which he is unfamiliar may include calamity. He must avoid the latter somehow, and so he begins to twist and turn and grope about in a blind, uncritical sort of way. Throughout his history he has seized upon one obvious explanation which lies close at hand and is as if provided for his very case. That explanation developed as follows.

Among the experiences of all men are certain illusions, where the brain conjures up figures which have no existence in the world of sane and waking realities. Such illusions cover what seems to be seen, heard, and felt in dreams, delirium, and other like states. The savage has no tests of reality upon which to judge that such sights, sounds, and other sensations are illusions. What he sees in these states are duplicates of living men, animals, and other realities; and he also sees the dead. In the last case he cannot be observing the bodies of the dead, for those he knows, at least in many instances, to have been entombed or destroyed. At death something evidently left the deceased person, and it must be that which he sees. These duplicates must be the breath that left the dying man when he "breathed his last," or expired ("breathed out"), or "gave up the ghost."

Without going into the matter more exhaustively, we may record that this ghostly duplicate of the dead was figured as possessing unlimited powers of ill which no human being could resist. The sentiment felt toward these ghosts was a searching fear unlike any fear of mere bodily harm; it was a ghastly, nocturnal terror that froze the blood. It was fear of supernatural power, and ghost-fear is as good a name for it as any other.

It was easy to leap to the conclusion that these spirits were the agents of all the otherwise inexplicable things in life, and particularly of all the ill fortune. But, whether easy or not, the jump was made by primitive peoples — not by a tribe here and there, but generally and over the whole earth. The savage peopled his world with a vast host of beings invisible, except on occasion, and in general maleficent and dangerous. This is the third environment, after the physical and social, to which adjustment had to be made by peoples to whom it was as real as either of the others. How, then, was such adjustment to be made?

It is necessary to understand that the ghosts retained the same nature as living men, as well as the same human form; the same wants and weaknesses — hunger, vanity, greed, and all the rest. The only difference was that they were much more powerful, and generally ill-willed and dangerous. They were nearest like a domineering, ill-natured chief; and the manner in which they were treated was the manner men had hit upon for handling potent and irritable human beings. There were really but two ways to get along with such a person: to avoid him or to please him; and men turned at once to the avoidance and propitiation of the spirit. Human beings were too weak to attack him unless they were helped by some other spirits which they might, by bribery, get on their side. Always it was necessary first to stand well with the most powerful spirits; then perhaps these might drive off the others or lend protection against their assaults. Avoidance, propitiation, and exorcism (" swearing away ") have been the stock methods of primitive peoples in dealing with the supernatural powers.

In carrying out these methods a number of devices or adjustments have been evolved. To avoid the continued presence of the ghosts of the dead, that is, to avoid being " haunted," the common method was abandonment of the dead body, or of the house or locality of death. The property of the dead was destroyed, lest he should come back after it, and for a long time after a man's death nobody dared marry his widow. His name was not mentioned, lest he think himself summoned to return. Relatives disguised themselves, so that he would not recognize them during his prowlings and fasten upon them. Numerous other customs of avoidance have been practised at different times and in different places by way of avoiding the ghosts and spirits. But perhaps we are better acquainted with the practices designed to please the supernatural powers and win their favor, for these are more obvious and general, lasting on into civilization.

Broadly speaking, these are all included under the term worship. If one savage wants to please another, or get something out of him, he offers a gift. Experience has taught him this way to favor; and believing that the spirits are like men, he applies the same method in dealing with them. Such gifts are "made sacred" to the spirits, that is, "sacrificed" to them. The most obvious satisfaction which can be offered, on a stage where every one is intent on the struggle for existence, is food; and we need not go beyond the Old Testament to show that food-offerings were once a prime method of securing spiritual approval and support. Since human flesh was eaten by a number of peoples, it was sacrificed also to their gods. But food is not the only gift possible. Clothing was sacrificed; and houses, in the form of temples, were built for the supernatural powers. In short, anything that men desired was a good sacrifice to the spirits. Men denied themselves in order to please the spirits; hence the sense of the word sacrifice as meaning self-denial.

Other things that pleased men were grand titles, and flattery in general; and so worship was full of adulation. Men liked sports and games; hence the funeral games, to delight the departing spirit, as in Homer and Vergil. Music pleased the human ear; hence the hymns to the spirits, and the use of drums and trumpets in religious ceremonies. Dancing is one of the chief delights of the savage; and so he organizes great religious dances. To catalogue the various sacrifices and ceremonies undertaken to win spiritual favor and help would be to list all the innumerable things and actions which please men. Anything that satisfies the eye, ear, palate, or nose of man will appeal to the senses of his gods. He can tickle their vanity or gratify their cupidity or revengefulness and acquire merit in so doing.

Still another form of pleasing the higher powers consists in subjecting one's self to pain and misery. It seems that the gods of the backward peoples do not like to see human beings happy. They like to have them go hungry and not have many pleasures. It is particularly dangerous for any man to have a run of good fortune, for the gods become jealous. Polycrates became nervous over his good luck, and tried to find out how to avoid consequent calamity. He was advised to throw away something he valued highly, as a sacrifice; and he cast a much-prized ring into the sea. The ring reappeared in the belly of a captured fish, the story goes, this indicating that his sacrifice was not accepted. Later, it is represented, his fortune turned, and he perished wretchedly.

To avoid the appearance of prosperity is the safe policy, with the gods as with a rapacious chief. So people pleased the spirits by fasting, by going naked or in rags, by renouncing the pleasures of life, by being serious instead of gay. They took vows to refrain from certain foods, to make long and tiresome pilgrimages; they tortured themselves by flogging, lying upon beds of spikes, and otherwise " mortifying the flesh." They turned all compliments aside, and called children whom they loved by names such as " puppy," or " dried monkey," so that the jealous spirits would not see their happiness and take it away.

Exorcism, as has been remarked, requires superhuman force; for man as mere man cannot expel or cast out the evil spirits that bring death, disease, and ill fortune. But one spirit can be won over and induced to assault and drive off another; and there are objects and substances which possess inexplicable powers, thought to be indwelling spirits, which can be used to get the same result. Such instrumentalities are called fetishes. Fire is a great fetish and so is water; and both are used to expel evil influences. Pain and disease are thought to be due to the presence of an evil spirit in the body; and the ailing person, or part of the body, is heated and burned, or bathed or steamed, in order to expel that spirit. Fumigation and the " water-cure " are practised, not for any reason that would strike us as sensible — certainly not for cleanliness — but for what we should call superstitious motives. Squeezing or rubbing the seat of pain (massage), the making of intolerable odors, and the administering of horrible doses of medicine — all these are common methods of driving off the evil spirits of disease. It will be noted that some of them are still used, and unquestionably secure relief; but the savage has no idea, as we have, of the real reason why they do that. He has discovered some real emetics and cathartics, but it was by accident, as he groped about and tried this and that. Selection between these variations has taken place, and he has, unawares, hit upon some real medicines.

Other fetishes that had power to expel evil spirits or to protect from them were amulets, talismans, and charms. The last were really songs (*carmina*) or spells — magic formulas, which generally invoked the power of some friendly spirit, thus frightening away the evil influence. The whole subject of magic comes in here, though magic is really outside of the professed religion and consists often in what was called, in the Middle Ages, " the black art," whereby wizards and witches gained the assistance of evil spirits, or even of the Devil, to assist their sinful purposes against pious people. Then the latter appealed to their own deity by quoting Scripture or making the sign of the cross, which put the devils to flight. Mystic power was seen also in certain numbers and in combinations of letters and signs — power which anyone could wield if he could get hold of the proper combinations, often senseless formulas such as " Open, Sesame! " or " Abracadabra."

It has been noted that men have always been very keen to get good luck and to avoid bad. One of the ways to do this was to know what was coming. And so there were developed many methods of forecasting the future, or divination. Of course no mere man could do that; the savage knows well enough that if anyone is to foresee coming events, these must be revealed to him by the spirits. But the latter have, it is believed, filled nature with signs and omens which need only to be correctly interpreted in order to prophesy. Such signs are very numerous; for instance, the flight and cries of birds, the behavior of animals, the movements of the heavenly bodies. The auspices ("inspection of birds") were taken by observation of peculiarities in the intestines of slain fowls; and we still speak of an enterprise as starting off "with good auspices," or "auspiciously." Comets were tremendous portents; and the function of astrology was prophecy by the stars. Horoscopes were taken to determine whether a proposed marriage would be fortunate or not; and this was no idle performance, for if the horoscope indicated ill fortune, the union was off for good. Prophets got themselves into a state of ecstasy by whirling, fasting, self-torture, and the use of poisons and " spirits "; then they were " possessed of a spirit," which revealed, through them as mouth-pieces, the complexion of the future.

In the Middle Ages, the Church was the recognized agency for dealing with strange and unpredictable calamities. Men were oppressed by fear of famines, diseases, storms, and floods, which were all due to evil spirits. Only the Church, by its connection with God, the great spirit that controlled all, could foresee and combat these. Hence the tremendous power of the Church — something without modern parallel, for we no longer feel the blind fears of the mediæval people. The Litany besought deliverance from lightning and from tempest, from pestilence, plague, and famine, from battle, murder, and sudden death.

To try to cover the whole subject of religious evolution, even in a large book, would be impossible; we are seeking here to suggest the main lines of adjustment to the supernatural environment, without citing much detail. But we can see, from what has gone before, the place which religion naturally and inevitably takes in the life of the race. It deals with all that which, though undoubtedly a factor in life, is beyond present knowledge; with forces that are known by experience to be present in the field, but which cannot be explained or calculated or dealt with by ordinary methods — not by such adjustments as men make to heat and cold, gravitation, or elasticity of materials. Since man can never have full knowledge, there will never be a time when the inexplicable is not present; in fact, since his knowledge will always remain slight in the face not only of all there is to know, but of all there is which he cannot hope to know, there will always be a host of mysteries which will remain unaccounted for except by reference to the supernatural.

Let the circle X represent the universe, which is an infinity of things, and is labelled with the sign of infinity. Let the dot in the center represent man. And let circles concentric at that dot represent man's knowledge of the universe at successive stages. Circle A stands for, let us say, a knowledge of how to generate fire, make simple tools, and do other things that a backward savage can do. All outside of A must be regarded by those within A as the province of the supernatural, that

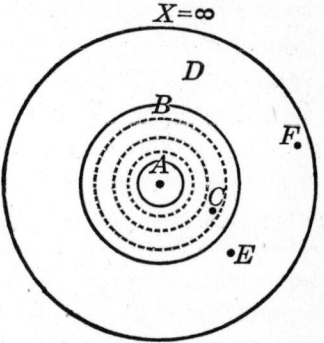

is, of religious explanation. But the circles (dotted) extend, as evolution goes on, to cover new areas, and things once referred to the supernatural, as C, a comet, became the objects of ordinary knowledge. Let circle B stand for all we know today. Then the belt D includes all we do not know; all which must remain unexplained unless it is referred to the supernatural.

Some things out there, such as E, the so-called canals of Mars, we hope to explain later on, just as we have explained C; so we do not call in the supernatural to account for it. But there are other things, such as F, the origin of life, which many of us have no hope of explaining. About such a matter most people would say: " It was created thus "; but that is a reference to the supernatural. It is to be noted that though the inner circles encroach upon the area of the outer one, X, they do not reduce it, for X is infinite, and you can take any finite quantity from infinity without diminishing it at all. In other words there is just as much room in the range referable to the supernatural as there ever was.

The great service of religion to early man was the discipline it enforced upon him. He was wild, freedom-loving, and lawless; but he had to become orderly and law-abiding as a condition of living on, or living better. Government did a good deal to reduce him to order; fear of punishment, that is, fear of human authority, held him in. If he was too unruly, he was executed and ceased to disturb other people; but generally he submitted through fear. However, human authority could be evaded; the chief was sometimes sick or asleep. Not so the ghosts and spirits, who were on the job all the time, night and day, year in and year out. And the fear of what the chief could do was as nothing beside the panic-fright of ghost-fear. The chief could beat a man or take away his belongings; but the spirits could, at a touch, turn him into a cripple, a loathsome leper, or even a hog or a toad, and could follow him up after death, in the spirit-world. Therefore, while he might contemplate evading the human authority, he dared not think of trying to overreach the spirits. So strong is the fear of the supernatural that strong young men have been known to die of fright upon the discovery that they had, unintentionally, broken some rule laid down in religion.

And religion lays down many and arbitrary rules. They are known as *taboos,* or prohibitions, in the form of " Thou shalt not." They forbid the eating of certain foods, labor at certain times, noise at others, the marrying of near kin, regicide, and a multitude of other things. They enforce labor, thrift, game-laws, war without and peace within, chastity, celibacy, fidelity between man and wife, and especially attendance on all the details of worship. They require obedience and more obedience, restrictions on personal freedom, self-sacrifice, renunciation of property and pleasure; and they generally discipline undeveloped man into something approaching a settled code of conduct — indeed, into a cast-iron code of conduct — so that he walks warily and carefully through life instead of thrashing and butting his way along, to the confusion of the community in which he lives.

Since the ancestors, when living, approved of the local ways of acting — the customary conduct — they continue, when they have become ancestral ghosts and gods, to guarantee them; only now their power is infinitely stronger and impossible to evade. Hence the ghost-fear which survivors feel for them is enlisted to support the customs and institutions of society. Thus is put behind the several blocks of customs that become institutions — marriage and the family, property, government, law — a tremendous engine of enforcement and sanction. As an adjustment, religion might be taken to be a sort of super-arrangement the presence of which makes all the rest more effective. And if religion performed no other service in its capacity as an institution of adjustment to life-conditions than the enforcement of an unbending, irresistible discipline, it would still represent one of the most successful adaptations ever evolved in society.

As time has passed, it has been refined and re-refined, like the other adjustments, at the hand of selection working upon constant variations. When any religious form has fallen out of adjustment, it has been at length removed, and something more expedient put in its place. Then that new form has been transmitted to succeeding generations and often to neighboring peoples. The sense of it remains always the same — namely, adjustment to the supernatural — but the superficial exhibitions of it have been carved and re-carved to harmonize with newly-arising conditions of society's life.

CHAPTER XI

THE ARTS OF PLEASURE

The types of adjustment hitherto considered — to the physical, the social, and the supernatural environment — are all serious business. Without them society would not be adjusted to its life-conditions, so as to live on. But when they have been attended to reasonably well, the pressure of life lets up somewhat, and there is leisure to spend upon lifting the plane of comfort. That is what man begins to struggle for when he has once caught sight of superior comforts that are to be had by the utilization of leisure won from the bare struggle for existence. Having assured himself of life, he reaches out after the possibility of living better. Having made sure of a sufficient quantity of food, he begins to think of luxuries and to strive for them. If he attains them, the next step is to regard them as matters of course; to shove them down, so to speak, into the list of necessities; and then to reach forward again. Sugar was once one of the greatest of luxuries in temperate regions; but now it is so much of a necessity that a nation which is cut off from sources of supply, say in war-time, is an object of sympathy, and other nations have even denied themselves to provide for the necessities of an ally thus stricken.

Every want that is satisfied breeds new desires, so that the process of straining toward more and better can never cease. It is not a question of mere living, we repeat, but of living upon a certain grade or according to a certain standard. The struggle for existence is no longer present under civilization, but is replaced by the struggle for a standard of living, which is being gradually elevated as time passes.

To maintain or raise this standard, men will work harder, will often deny themselves necessities, and will limit the size of their families. They want something more than basic animal satisfactions. Just where they may be said to be seeking for pleasure rather than mere satisfaction is difficult to say; but there are certainly a number of activities and instrumentalities in society that aim at nothing very practical. Without attempting to analyze the matter too closely, we can yet distinguish certain activities of societies which result in *self-gratification* rather than in self-maintenance. It is well to consider the simple origins of these, for they are occupying a larger place in social life all the time. Some of them need only to be mentioned, while others are worth considerable study.

Athletic sports and games are by no means unrepresented among savages, though it is often hard to distinguish them from the drill for war. Boat-racing, in similar manner, is partly practice in view of more serious purposes. But there are pure games, some of which have been adopted, like lacrosse, by civilized men. Pastimes of various sorts, resting upon a display of dexterity — for instance, complicated sets of string-tricks or cat's-cradle — provide hours of amusement. Corresponding mental gymnastics are offered by exercise on riddles; and the recounting of exploits, together with the telling of stories and myths, represents a favorite means of satisfying imagination and curiosity.

Special gratification of the senses is the object of much eager endeavor. Anything that will tickle the sense of taste, especially if it relieves the dull monotony of an almost unseasoned diet, is sought for with enthusiasm. Condiments like salt and spices of all sorts, and sweets, honey in particular, have appealed to men throughout history. The wide demand for the spices of the East outdistanced the call for mere nutritious food. Much history has been enacted about the trade in spices between West and East, for men would make a strong effort to get luxuries when they were not lured to strive for necessities.

Intoxicants also have appealed widely to mankind. Whenever people have been in possession of a substance from which an intoxicant could be derived, they have almost always learned to derive it; and traders have catered industriously to the taste for opium, alcohol, tobacco, stimulants, and narcotics, both strong and mild. Some writers have noted that work could be got out of the native by offering intoxicants, when no other inducement would avail. Not only that, but those who received their wages in whiskey quickly drank it up, and so returned to work sooner than the ones who were paid in less perishable commodities. In the case of condiments and intoxicants it is plainly not the food-value that counts, but the pleasurable sensation.

There is no manner of doubt, again, that the most backward of men are much interested in what we call the artistic. They like brilliance and color, and it evidently diverts them to draw figures or even simple patterns. Brass wire, mirrors, bright beads, and trinkets in general have served the trader as means of securing costly furs, ivory, rubber, and other valuable commodities. Many tribes paint the body or the tent or the totem-pole in gaudy colors; or they decorate the skin with tattoo-patterns in color, or embroider the clothing with threads or feathers of bright hue. The Pacific Islanders decked themselves with flowers. Even the men of the Ice Age drew representations of animals in their caves and the Bushmen of Africa made drawings on rocks. These were sometimes colored in a manner to appeal even to the civilized man. Sculpture was begun in the remote past by the carving out of rude figures of animals and men. Evidently early man was so constituted that he took great pleasure in making representations of what he saw about him. Through ages he kept on using his leisure time in such manner and thus laid the foundation of the several fine arts. All this was done, in good part, merely to please the eye.

There was also great enthusiasm for that which pleased the

ear. Primitive music impresses us generally as monotonous and uninteresting; but it was not so to the earliest performers or to their audiences. There is much singing among savages, especially in Africa; and musical instruments run all the way from the tom-tom up to wind, friction, and percussion devices of some complication. More or less connected with music is tale-telling — the recounting of legends and adventures. It is generally done in a more or less sing-song manner, and sometimes accompanied with music. It passes easily into poetry. The poet is supposed to " sing," and his professional instrument is the lyre. The Iliad begins with " Sing, goddess, the wrath of Achilles," and the Æneid copies this method of beginning: *Arma virumque cano,* " I sing of arms and of a man."

Another pleasing sensation was rhythm, which appealed chiefly to the ear but also set the body into motion. Dancing is one of the most popular enjoyments of backward peoples; but their dances are often not at all beautiful to us, even when we have adopted them for the sake of novelty or for some other non-artistic reason. The primitive dances are wild and exhausting, resulting in vertigo and even in paroxysms; but they are rhythmic. They are religious in object, as well as merely exciting and recreational; the spirits like to see them. They are also accompanied by singing and chanting, and it is out of the dance-rhythms that many of the older meters of poetry have developed; for the voice and the body kept time. The arsis (" lifting ") and thesis (" setting down ") of the poetic " foot " recall this line of development.

Further, the dance usually enacted some scene out of hunting, for instance, or out of war; the buffalo-dance and the war-dance were representations of what men did. Imitation went to the extent of reproducing animal cries, snarls, and grunts, and also human shouts and speech. The life of some god or hero might be acted out while it was being recounted by word of mouth. From such a performance to a rude sort of drama the distance is short. Leaders in the dance became actors, and the rest formed the chorus — for " chorus " means, in its origin, only a dance or a band of dancers. Thus out of the dance were developed the theater and acting — sources of recreation and pleasure which have blessed many generations of men. Music, poetry, and play-acting were all intertwined at the outset and have never been completely separated during their evolution.

But it is to be noted that they developed and were adjusted to their function of pleasing mankind, little by little, out of very rude beginnings. Variations sprang up and were tried out; then they were dropped or continued according as they met the taste of the age; and the forms that were most satisfactory were transmitted to succeeding stages. In some places and times all actors were masked and no women were permitted to act. Certain forms of music, literature, and histrionic art, like certain styles in painting and sculpture, gave way to others; but the general line of development is marked by a series of forms derived out of preceding forms, which is comparable in all essentials to an animal-series representative of the course of organic evolution.

In a preceding lesson the importance and seriousness in human life of the luck element have been referred to. People were, we saw, always afraid of ill luck, and always trying somehow to dodge or to win over the spirits that controlled chance. But just as men have always liked to play with the destructive element of fire, so, in far greater degree, have they taken pleasure in toying with luck. Savages have athletic games, as we have seen, and sometimes these are played purely for the physical pleasure in them; but there is usually a good deal of betting on the result. In fact, no game is a real game to the savage, or indeed to a good many persons living under civilization, if it does not include the element of gambling. Of course, the winner likes to get the stake for the sake of its value; but the real excitement often lies, after all, in the turn of luck — in the hazard rather than in the reward, in the process of appeal to chance rather than in the result, in uncertainty rather than certainty.

The uncertainty of a game or a bet is the interesting thing about it. Betting on a sure thing may satisfy greed, but not the gaming or sporting spirit. And the uncertainty is there, despite all preliminary estimating and forecasting. It is the ignorance of all the possible influencing conditions that lets in the element of chance. No one wants to wager with an opponent that the latter cannot break a window-pane with a hammer, for he knows that it can be done unless the performer falls dead or is suddenly paralyzed before he can strike; but he would hesitate to bet his all that a superior player could beat an inferior in a billiard game on any particular day. The best performer has his " day off "; and there is always a chance that that day will coincide with an inferior player's red-letter day, when he completely outplays himself; when the balls " will not roll " for the one, while they are always offering " set-ups " to the other.

Men have always liked to dally with this element of chance — this play of the unreckonable and unpredictable. It becomes a veritable passion. If he can do no better, a confirmed gambler will wager with himself, right hand against left. And most savages are inveterate gamesters. His fighting-cock is the joy of the Malay's life, and he will wager anything he has on a cock-fight, first stripping himself of all he wears, then staking wife and children and at last his own freedom. Slavery resulting from gambling-debts is not at all unheard-of. Gambling-devices begin with mere sticks or pebbles, to be hidden in the hand and their location guessed, and develop to include quite complicated apparatus; and where there is nothing to go on, the subtlety of the guessing ranges all the way from chance choice, as in the drawing of lots, to combinations where it is possible to use a great deal of intelligent inference and balancing of probabilities before facing the final alternatives. The joy of the game enters into many forms of self-maintenance that are not pure gambling, though sometimes a considerable element of the latter is thinly disguised as " speculation."

Another quite different type of pleasure-seeking results in the satisfaction of vanity and of the craving for ostentation. There are two things which men strive mightily to attain: uniformity with others and difference from others. The first spares one from unenviable distinction, while the latter sets him off in some enviable superiority. In the former case, he follows fashion; in the latter, he departs from the ordinary. Always there are appearing variations in dress and in behavior which either take hold or do not take hold. If they do, then people make great efforts not to seem behindhand; for if they do fall behind, they must expect humiliation and ridicule. It is part of a person's vanity or self-respect not to straggle behind his fellows in this matter of fashion. He is spurred, at any rate, to keep up with the crowd; and if he does, he feels a satisfaction that is very real.

The other aspect of the case is where one's vanity leads him to try to set himself above or apart from others, so as to receive admiration. This might be called pride. In any case, it is one of the most powerful of human sentiments, and it drives men to the most strenuous effort. Such exhibition of superiorities is what we call ostentation, and it takes a multitude of forms. It is said that when men have, by strict self-discipline, sought to banish all pride and be humble, yet pride slips in, in spite of them; for when they have ceased to be vain about everything else, they are proud of their humility. Some of the most arrogant of men have been ascetics who have stripped themselves of their possessions and become beggars and who have remained dirty and in rags; but they have often done this to show their lofty contempt for things most men prize, and they have been insufferably proud of their reputation for holiness.

The forms of ostentation exhibited by savages are often very childlike. They begin by operations on the body. The head is forced into a certain shape by pressure exerted upon the skulls of small children; the feet are cramped until they become well-nigh useless for locomotion; the nails are allowed to grow to great lengths, and the consequent uselessness of the hands is an indication that their possessor does not have to work for a living. The body is actually mutilated, by the knocking out of teeth, the filing of teeth to a point, the removal of hair, and the scarring of flesh. The German students used to be proud of the disfigurements they had attained by sword-cuts and kept the wounds on their faces open so that they would leave prominent scars after healing. The most artistic of all such bodily ornamentation is tattooing, an exceedingly painful operation but one which all wanted done; for often no girl could be married until she was tattooed and no boy was really a man until the patterns were complete. In the case of the finest tattooing, the naked body does not appear naked but as if clothed in delicate garments of the finest hue and pattern. The lips and gums were often tattooed so as to be purple; in such case any one who had red gums and lips was regarded as an uncouth and animal-like, low-caste person, while the most highly decorated were admired and accorded a high social position.

Much attention has been given to the hair. Sometimes the head is shaved, as a whole or in patterns, and all the body-hair, including eyebrows and eyelashes, is pulled out. Again, hairiness is admired, and the utmost pains are taken to build up an elaborate coiffure, often by mixing clay, grease, and other substances in the hair so as to make of it a hard, stiff, upstanding mass, which is then carved into eccentric shapes. The beard is regarded by some as a great ornament and is carefully cherished. False hair is common; horse-hairs are braided into the natural strands, and the whole is elaborately colored.

If, now, we leave the ornamental treatment of the body, and go forward to consider actual ornament, we find we have entered upon a chapter of great length and importance in human history. Savages who are otherwise naked adorn the body wherever ornament can be attached. Ears and nose are pierced to admit of the attachment of heavy rings and rods, and lips are perforated to admit plugs, called labrets. The legs are not seldom so weighed down with rings of metal that the wearer can barely shuffle along. The discomfort is as nothing compared with the gratification of seeing others admire and envy; the case is like that of a person suffering agonies from overtight ornamental shoes, perhaps with lofty heels, but happy all the same. Some Africans will wind about the body, for show, all the cloth they own. On a hot, tropical day, they nearly roast, and may be so enveloped that their arms stand almost straight out, but their pleasure in the sensation they create is by no means diminished. It is heightened rather; for their very bodily discomfort is proof of their wealth and power.

Where ornament is merely hung on the body, it is naturally suspended from one of two places, the neck or the waist; and it is generally in front, where the owner can see and enjoy it. It is often insufficient to hide the body, but there is no so-called "sense of shame." The sense of shame is connected largely with the feeling that one is not covered as others are — one may be much ashamed of his bare hands where all the rest are wearing white gloves — and, since nearly all who are covered at all are covered in front just below the waist, a special sense of shame generally attaches, among clothed peoples, to that part of the body. As the habit of going about fully clothed develops, the sense of shame seems to spread to cover nudity of most parts of the body.

The fact is that among many peoples of the earth clothing, such as it is, is almost wholly ornamental; so that we can conclude, especially if we believe that man must have developed originally in the warm climates, that clothing came for the most part out of vanity. A good bit of it is still worn for show and not for any particular reason other than that; for instance, furs in summer and thin and flimsy materials in winter.

Many garments are uncomfortable, but there is no thought of refusing to wear them for that reason, provided they are fashionable or ostentatious. Some varieties are actually unhygienic, for instance, skirts that drag on the ground to gather up filth and germs; and if a hygienic fashion is adopted there is no guarantee that it will last long.

The pride of wealth and possessions is a driving factor of great power, and the rich have always disported themselves in a satisfied consciousness of the envy of the rest. Especially do those to whom the sensation of affluence is unfamiliar—the so-called " newly-rich "— endeavor to impress their importance upon all observers. Pride of family leads to a variety of efforts to find or to invent a genealogy, and to arrogant habits, as of a race conscious of its superior qualities. This vanity of all those who have " arrived " in society is constantly tickled by recognition of that fact in the newspapers and also by the enthusiasm of those who are still striving to arrive. Many games are played, in wealth-getting and social climbing, with the pleasure in prospect of being admired and envied.

All this has been so for ages past, and the savage warrior is just as proud of his eagle-feathers, each of which represents some notable exploit, as any modern fighter of his decorations. All men have been eager to win a prestige which should set them off from the rest so that people might point them out as notables. High-minded men will toil all their lives, endure pain and hardship, sacrifice most of the pleasures of life, and finally wear themselves out untimely, for the sake of ambition and in order to leave a name behind them. They take their pleasure in a prospect which, in many cases, as even they must know, cannot be realized till after their death. Benjamin Franklin spoke of " the pest of glory "; and he meant by that the pest of a vanity which does not hesitate to sacrifice the real and general interests of a nation for the prospect of winning the admiration and applause of others.

It can be seen that the various methods of getting pleasure, over and above the mere satisfaction of hunger and other basic needs, take up a goodly share of human effort. Whatever time and energy the savage has left over, after attending to his immediate necessities, he spends in pleasure-getting; and with the development of civilization and the progressive emancipation of men from the mere struggle for existence, it is possible to devote more and more time to the pursuit of gratifications of one kind and another. It is possible to cater more copiously and successfully to lower desires and passions or to develop more refined types of enjoyment corresponding to refined tastes. One of the higher developments of civilization is pleasure in hard work; there are many men who, through a lifetime of endeavor, have acquired such a taste for activity of body or mind that they are utterly miserable in idleness. It is needless to say that such a condition represents a great change from the state of mind of the savage.

It is possible to regard the arts of pleasure as a set of adjustments to conditions permitting leisure. But if the leisure is employed in a torpid manner, as in sleep or aimless loafing, evidently not much is made of it for society's benefit. A more expedient adjustment is where mere animal gratification is replaced by further stimuli, where ever-new wants are evolved and call for redoubled effort in getting satisfaction for them. With the new needs and new satisfactions, life assumes greater scope and intensity. Lower motives take on refinement, as when mere vanity works out into a sense of honor and self-respect; and satisfactions become correspondingly less crude. It is well for any society if its members are not content with crude pleasures; no matter how simple they may be, satisfactions need not be coarse and brutal. Appreciation of line and color, of music, of the marvels of science, of the sublimities of religion, has always gone with the rest of the adjustments that characterize high culture. Not unjustly has a refined taste for such pleasures been called the flower of civilization.

CHAPTER XII

SCIENCE AND ART

In the chapter on Religion it was pointed out that even the lowest savage acts in a manner which we call sensible and reasonable in cases where he has knowledge enough to do so; and that it is only because of his ignorance that he goes off into magic and other practices which we call superstitions. He knows very little, and we know, relatively to him, a great deal; so that between his stage of evolution and ours there has been a considerable increase of knowledge. This chapter has to do with that evolution. The pace at which advance in knowledge has proceeded has been quite unequal; for many ages it was very slow, but has been immensely accelerated within the last couple of centuries.

So long as men merely reacted upon experience, not seeking into the causes of things except in so far as they referred the unknown to the supernatural, there could be little acquisition of real knowledge. And yet it was precisely because of the, to us, superstitious ideas which men held that they were spurred on to the discovery of those laws which underlie the phenomena of nature and of society. Only when they caught sight of the laws did they come into the range of science. It might be put this way: no science without laws; no laws without a comparison of many cases; no record of cases without observation; no observation without interest; no interest without emotion — and, in many cases, no interest without superstitious fear. You have got to start with some emotion, for there was no such thing as scientific curiosity. It is entirely possible that the fear was not always terror before the supernatural; it might well have been fear of hunger that led men to learn, for instance, the habits of animals; but since the unknown was so regularly referred to the supernatural, it is evident that fear of the unknown, which led to observation, and at length, to understanding, was an important driving factor. And that fear, as we have seen, was more powerful than almost any other emotion that men felt.

It is time to illustrate. At an early stage in human progress men became convinced that the stars governed human destiny. That was a false start; but let us see how it worked out, by correction, into truth. If the stars governed destiny, it was plainly necessary to study them, and men did so earnestly. After a while they noticed that similar combinations of the heavenly bodies turned up at regular periods, and by comparison of observations, were able, at length, to predict such events as eclipses. They did not know the why of an eclipse, but they knew when to expect it. They gradually learned that the stars did not move arbitrarily or whimsically, but with regularity; that there were laws that ruled their movements. Further study revealed the constant operation of law and order throughout the starry universe, and men were getting behind the scenes, so to speak. But if the stars moved in accord with law, they could not be real spirits, able to interfere with human destiny. Only such heavenly bodies as comets, whose coming and going were a riddle, could be that; and the belief in the effect of comets on human affairs lasted on for a long time after that in the influence of planets had begun to fade away. The irregular remained ominous long after the regular had ceased to be so. Of course the ignorant held to the old beliefs, which were engendered in ignorance, the longest.

Yet if it had not been for the belief in the influence of the stars on human life, there would have been no strong motive for observation of the heavenly bodies. We know now that the presence of the mosquito has had an important influence upon human well-being; but the savage did not think that, and so he spent no time on the study of this insect. Out of the conviction about the stars, which we reject, came, however, the endless observations of, say, the Chaldæan shepherds, and then, in the fullness of time, and in the light of these observations, a science. The old set of beliefs led to astrology and the casting of horoscopes; while out of the knowledge finally gained as the result of long observation has come the science of astronomy (" star-law "), with power to predict the position of the heavenly bodies and even to attain such practical results as the constructions of tide-almanacs.

The same course of events took place in the development of chemistry out of alchemy, and of medicine out of magic. In both cases there was at the outset a lively emotion, either of fear or some other, which led to observation and re-observation, and at length to the correction, not only of minor details, but of the whole original theory. So, one might say, science has in these and other cases risen out of superstition, and but for that superstition might have been indefinitely retarded in its development.

With these facts in mind, let us now endeavor to get some idea of that acceleration of pace in the acquisition of knowledge which, as we have noted, is a relatively modern phenomenon. Man has been on earth a great many thousands of years. He set out on his career by making adjustments in a hit-or-miss sort of way but, because he had a degree of intelligence that beasts had not, his experience resulted in knowledge. It was derived from practical experience and resulted, even in its highest development, in rules of thumb. Yet it was knowledge, though unclassified and unorganized. As the race developed, this fund of information slowly accumulated and was imperfectly transmitted by word of mouth from generation to generation; because it was in a number of little, disconnected heaps, in the possession of small, disconnected groups of men, it could not be subjected to much comparison, criticism, and selection.

On this stage it remained a long time. Then came the development of communication between the small tribal groups, chiefly by intermarriage and trade; thus ideas were brought into competition for wider acceptance; and there ensued a mutual borrowing of knowledge by which the store of each of two neighboring groups became the store of both. This is sometimes called the cross-fertilization of culture, and it greatly promotes the rate of growth of knowledge. It must be understood that most of the many thousands of years of the race's history were taken up in getting as far as this. If mankind has been on earth no more than two or three hundred thousands of years, yet when about twenty-four twenty-fifths of that time had elapsed, they had yet to develop adequate means for such regular transmission of ideas and knowledge, over space and through time, as to admit of wide comparison and selection of ideas, and of stimulation to further acquisition.

Somewhere about ten or fifteen thousand years ago there entered into the situation an almost if not quite indispensable adjustment for the dissemination and accumulation of knowledge, and that was the invention of the art of recording, that is, of writing with an alphabet. To get laws there must be a comparison of cases. But numerous cases did not occur at one and the same time, or at one and the same place. Where there was no way of recording them except in memory and tradition, there could be no effective comparison. Events are generally much altered in the telling, especially if oral tradition has to cover considerable intervals of time. But when people could set down the facts while they were fresh in mind, the record was not only much more trustworthy, but included details that could not but be lost in their passage through the minds and mouths of a series of oral recounters. It also lacked the imaginary elements that all tale-tellers are sure to introduce as embroidery calculated to enhance the wonder-element in their stories. Some form of writing — and the more perfected it was, the better for the truth — enabled men to store, accumulate, and compare observations, and so to apprehend the regularities and the laws that underlay the observable phenomena. This is one of the reasons why the invention of writing is reckoned among the very most important and fundamental exploits of man; for so much that came later rests on it as on a foundation-stone. Of course, with the invention of printing the possibility opened up by writing, of transmitting ideas and knowledge over both space and time, and so of speeding up the process of learning, was augmented many fold.

But mere transmission of ideas, though it brought different types of them into competition, with the result of winnowing out the ones which tested up best upon experience and of considerably speeding up the increase of quantity and quality of knowledge, was not the agency which accelerated the knowledge-gaining process to its modern rate of speed. That was the development of science, with its methods for prying into the very marrow of things. Of the two to three thousand centuries of man's life on earth all but the last two had passed away before the so-called "century of science," which we call the nineteenth, was at hand. Thus, while the recorded history of mankind is very short as compared with his whole history, the length of the scientific age, as compared with that of recorded history, has been still shorter — and covers, in fact, only about one one-hundredth of that period. And yet that age has done, in its relatively brief span of time, more for the attainment of the sort of knowledge men need in adjusting to life-conditions than all the preceding ages put together. Science constitutes the latest great conquest in the campaign of adjustment.

We have noticed heretofore that men have been led to observe and compare facts and experiences by the very necessity of living, but that they did that for long ages in an unsystematic and uncertain sort of way. They drew their conclusions from too few instances — sometimes from no more than one or two — and often would continue to act in accord with such snap-judgments after they had been suffering for some time from their original adoption of a faulty principle. If they had suffered sufficiently, they would at length change their actions, and then try to justify that change by interpreting their principle so that it would cover their new policy. Thus were corrections made at the hand of sad experience. Now what science aims to do is to abbreviate this clumsy process and to obviate the suffering. It tries, first of all, to get at the right principle immediately, and then to test out its applications by experiment, not waiting for correction at the hand of daily experience, but correcting itself as it goes along. It does not turn a process loose in the world to see if it will work, that is, if it will constitute a good adjustment; it does not turn it loose till it has been proved to work in the laboratory or elsewhere.

Its method in all this is simply a systematized and organized edition of what men have always done in dealing with situations that confront them. If they have solved them in the past, it has been, we say, because of common-sense. Science is common-sense exercised more carefully upon more copious material — on many cases instead of a few. The scientist first gathers what Darwin called " a good body of facts." Science always starts thus, with feet solidly upon the ground. Next all these facts are weighed, compared, and classified. They are so arranged that they can be viewed in their relations with one another. Then the collector tries to frame some explanation, or theory, that will explain all or most of them.

If he sees one that seems to do that, he accepts it for the time, but proceeds to test it out upon more facts or by actual experiment; and if it continues to work, he gets more faith in it. Perhaps then he publishes it, and the rest of the scientists compare it with other men's theories and apply it to other sets of facts which they know about. Flaws are picked in it, and betterments are suggested. If it weathers the storm, it is accepted until a better one is proposed. Sometimes a scientist will see several possible explanations (multiple hypotheses) and, to decide between them, must wait until they can be tested out in some way. There was once a scientist who constructed several possible explanations of the meteor-showers in the fall. Calculators were set to work to see which hypothesis would work out. All failed to verify except one, but that did and was presently accepted by all.

At first men met the details of life-conditions each for itself, learning from experience how to meet them. But when they had come to know the laws behind natural manifestations, and had begun to get a perspective of nature, they did not need to flounder so hopelessly in detail but could deal with life-conditions in sets, as it were, and could even predict to some degree what was to be expected, and get ready for it. That means that they had come to possess a power of adjustment, or pre-adjustment, much superior to anything which they had had before. The mind had been furnished with a conception of the orderliness of the universe, and of a relation of means to ends, which enabled it to execute its reactions upon life-conditions with much more intelligence, rapidity, and precision. It approached new conditions not merely in the light of isolated experiences, but with the ability to classify the cases presented and with a general knowledge of how to deal with the classes of cases. This meant a saving of the time and effort formerly spent in fumbling about. Men learned how to size up a new situation, and where to take hold in adjusting to it.

This is illustrated, day by day, in the world about us. An iron plate has buckled, and the ignorant workman attacks the bulge with his hammer, striving to pound it down; but the result is further buckling elsewhere and the spoiling of the plate. The man who knows about the stresses in the iron, however, begins to pound elsewhere than upon what looks, at first sight, to be the seat of trouble, and presently the plate is flattened out and ready for use. Again, the ignorant person strives to cure boils by poultices or rheumatism by local treatment merely, where the doctor, who is more deeply versed in knowledge of the human body and its processes, prescribes a tonic or a diet. The tendency of ignorance is to treat symptoms, whereas real knowledge of underlying conditions and laws leads to an assault on the disease itself. Similarly in the social field: much effort used once to be expended on fixing prices at what was considered to be a " just " level; but the instructed economist knows that prices are secondary matters, or symptoms, whereas the law of supply and demand is the fundamental and governing factor. The ignorant person is likely to blame all his woes upon the " government " and to vote against the party in power; whereas his troubles, upon scientific examination, turn out to be due to his own foolish actions, or to any one or more of a dozen other conditions much more fundamental than the holding of office by any particular set of men. To be able to identify true and fundamental causes is certainly an advantage in living.

It was noted above that the invention of writing and printing greatly speeded up the knowledge-getting process; and if that was so, it can easily be imagined what an acceleration was derived from the development of such an instrument as scientific method. For through it science has revealed the very underlying key-processes and laws of nature. And science runs little risk of becoming set and dogmatic in its ways, for it provides for its own correction by rival experimentation and theorizing, and it is always being brought back to test upon observable fact. It is a fair inference from the immediate past that we must look forward to a progressive speeding-up in the accumulation of knowledge, at the hand of science. This puts a special burden upon members of society to keep up with the game. The ignoramus can do more harm now than ever before by stupidly thrashing about in the neighborhood of society's intricate, high-powered, and high-speeded machinery.

Science is really man's most highly developed instrument for adjustment. Because it has secured such successes in meeting life-conditions, the notion has become widespread that man is lord of nature, and that he is not required to adjust to environment, but adjusts the environment to himself. If he does not like an isthmus where nature has put it, he makes a strait instead. If he prefers a smooth, hard surface to the one nature has provided, he lays down asphalt or concrete. But this is simply moving things about. If he " makes " Portland cement, he is really only bringing together certain constituents whose natural qualities he cannot change any more than he can halt the sun. The fact is that he gets his results by clever adjustments to things as they are; and the development of science is what has enabled him to know how things are. The laws of their nature, of their combinations, and all the rest, are dug out by long and painful labors in the laboratories and libraries; and then may come the scientific applications. But nothing can be done that is contrary to the original nature of things.

In the course of time men have come to take a great interest in the way things work and are, in the universe, entirely apart from any practical considerations. That scientific curiosity, which the savage did not have, has been developed in the most refined minds into a veritable passion. Pasteur spent a long time and much effort in the endeavor to find out whether life was or was not spontaneously generated out of dead matter. This is what is known as the pursuit of " pure theory." There is a common belief that theory is unpractical. It is not, if it is arrived at by scientific methods. It is, on the contrary, the most practical of all things, for it represents the broadest and most comprehensive sets of truths. Unless you have theory, there is nothing to guide practice — indeed, there may even be nothing to put into practice. Pasteur settled the case of spontaneous generation by proving that it does not occur; but directly out of his highly theoretical studies issued the explanation of the fermentation of foods and drinks, and of the infection of wounds; and, at length, the methods for preventing both evils. In all cases science informs us as to just what it is that we must adjust to, so that we can make adjustments with more intelligence and success. What we have to adjust to is something we cannot alter, but if we know just what to expect — or even approximately what to expect — we are immeasurably more likely to succeed in our adaptation than if we went at it blindly and hit-or-miss.

It is a fancy of some people to belittle science because it cannot explain all things, such as the origin of life; or because it has made errors in the past or present; or because it presents its conclusions with some uncertainty and caution. Theories are contemptuously referred to as " guesses." But science has never claimed that it could explain the unknowable; and even if such problems as the origin of life an be solved, science does not expect to be able to solve them yet awhile. To blame science for not explaining these problems, which it does not set out to explain, is like scolding a carpenter because he cannot tune a piano — he makes no claim to do that. As for the errors of science, they are natural enough, and science knows it; unlike some other truth-revealing agencies, science makes constant provision for its own correction and is ready to weigh all objections and criticisms. Because it knows how hard is the discovery of the truth, it does not claim infallibility. That is the reason also why it states its findings with reserve and caution. Anyone who criticizes science for such caution is really finding fault with honesty.

And as for " guesses," there are several kinds of guess. One is where the guesser knows little or nothing, and his opinion is a mere shot in the dark. Another is where he has for years studied the subject, gathered thousands of cases in evidence, and balanced all the pros and cons a hundred times over. At length he allows himself to infer as to the significance of his hard-won knowledge. If this is a guess, it is so different from the ordinary variety that it deserves a separate name. That name is " theory " or " hypothesis," and only ignorance or willful misrepresentation will confuse it with common guess-work.

Scientists have to use their imagination, as poets do, but they use it on the results of laborious investigation, not on the empty air. The "happy thoughts" of a scientist come from having filled his mind with facts and brooded over them until, in some fortunate hour, their relation under law suddenly occurs to him. It could not have occurred to other than a well-stocked and strictly-disciplined mind.

Disputing over a thing never settles the question of its worth. Talk is cheap. It is demonstration that a thing works that carries real persuasion. Well, science has certainly demonstrated; and it has demonstrated so well that its very detractors, while they are assaulting it, are living by it.

The very people who seek to belittle science — and they are generally those who would prefer to hold to the superstitions out of which science has painfully worked — depend upon it, in sickness and in health, for life and comfort. It is an age of science, and without it the highest civilizations could not have reached their present level, and could not, having reached it, sustain it. The person who affects to despise science rides in trains whose service to him is rendered possible by science, eats scientifically prepared foods, drinks "pasteurized" or otherwise scientifically guaranteed milk, calls in at need a doctor whose whole training is impossible except for science, and prints his assaults on science on machines and by processes for which science is responsible. To despise science is often a mere pose, taken by people who wish to be considered æsthetic. It is doubtful if any of those who rave romantically over the marvels of the universe have anything more than a superficial idea of those wonders. Nature does not reveal herself to the casual onlooker. The scientist with insight and imagination is too deeply impressed to rave. Denial of the cultural value of science is a damaging admission. In any case, we live by science. It may not be perfect but, such as it is, it represents the best we have to go by in dealing with most of the life-conditions that surround us.

It is probably unnecessary to catalogue the triumphs of science in dealing with the physical environment. By knowing beforehand the nature of materials and forces, we have been able to turn minerals, plants, and animals to our advantage in the battle of life. Once the sea was a perilous barrier; now it is a means of communication. We are called upon daily to note progress in the conquest of the air. Every year the scientists are shooting closer to the bull's-eye in the understanding, prevention, and cure of disease. Mental hygiene, no more than dreamed of a little while back, is now a commonplace. Where scientific methods can be applied there is always hope of the solution of difficulties. Problems may be presented to science which it is, for a long time, unable to solve; but every instructed person expects that they will ultimately yield. Science " hath her victories." But this does not mean that science can explain everything. Spencer divided all things into the knowable and the unknowable, and noted that science was concerned only with the former.

If the student has caught the point of a preceding lesson (ch. X), he will realize that, with all our science, our ignorance must remain for all time endless; and that what we cannot explain and have no hope of explaining will continue to be referred to the supernatural. The supernatural environment is beyond the power of science to investigate; it is the region of faith. But this is no reason why science should not press on and do what it can. If the race had refused to try to find out what it could, by experience and study, at a time when nearly everything was referred to the supernatural and to faith, then it would have remained in barbarism and superstition. The fact is that the race had to go ahead toward science as a condition of its persistence and comfort, and in so doing had to drop many of its supernatural explanations.

This did no harm to religion — unless one means by religion the original and uncouth product. As we have seen in the chapter just referred to, religion has become a more and more refined adjustment as grosser and mistaken beliefs have been discredited by the advance of knowledge. But for science, most of those grosser beliefs would have persisted. Truth is not inconsistent with truth; and we know that the tested findings of science are true — at any rate, true enough to be necessary for life. If, then, religion is truth, it cannot conflict with science — not in its essentials, that is. The reason for the idea that science and religion are inconsistent lies in the fact that the former has upset not a few pet doctrines of the latter. If doctrines are all there is to religion, then science and religion are inconsistent; and so, for that matter, and even within the very body of religion, are the various sects inconsistent with one another. But if the essence both of science and of religion is to seek and know the truth, then they are in essential harmony. If religion sticks to the scientifically unknowable, that is, to the ultimate mysteries of existence which it alone can claim to know, there is no chance of any collision with science.

Several of the many conquests of science have been alluded to in a recent paragraph; but they were the exploits of only one group of sciences, called the *natural sciences* because they deal directly with nature, as compared with those which have to do with human society — the *social sciences*. The natural sciences have had for a number of years a favored position in men's estimation because of the long and rapid succession of important services which they have rendered to human well-being. Of the natural sciences, chemistry and physics are fundamental, for the former studies the very elements out of which matter, both inorganic and organic, is formed, and the latter investigates the forms of motion or energy that exist in the world. Matter and motion are basic phenomena, and it is readily seen that an understanding of the laws that govern the combinations of chemical elements and the qualities of motion dig deep under the ancient and scrappy knowledge of this or that substance and of some few forms of energy and motion.

Life itself is the object of study of another fundamental

science, biology; but life manifests itself in matter and in motion, and so biology is commonly thought of as a derived science. The theory of the adjustment of life to life-conditions, advanced by Darwin, is a biological theory. In general, biology deals with living organisms, and so, in a broad sense, includes anatomy, physiology, and a number of other sub-sciences that deal with living beings. Astronomy is another derived science, which centers on the nature and motions of the heavenly bodies. Geology deals with the construction of the earth. Both astronomy and geology derive general laws revealing the existence of orderliness throughout space and time. Mathematics furnishes a method applicable to any science which yields facts and relations that can be measured; it is indispensable to the pursuit of the deeper problems of physics, chemistry, and astronomy, and has its applications in biology and geology.

This is not the place in which to describe the natural sciences except in the most general manner. But the reader can readily see that the discovery of the controlling laws about matter, motion, and life confers upon man a widened knowledge of conditions to which, though he cannot change them at all, he can at least adjust himself with his eyes open, instead of stumbling about in peril, like a person in a dark room full of live wires. He knows, at least, now that the light of science has been let in, where some of the wires are; and he has learned how to avoid them, or even how to put to his own use the fearful powers which they carry. There are similar currents in the life of society — but around them a Cimmerian night has brooded for untold ages, and common-sense in dealing with them has never been well trained or organized.

Up to very recent years there has been no real application of scientific method to the study of human society. The natural sciences have flourished and have reached results in practical application which are loudly and justly applauded; but the social sciences have not kept pace and have not won anything like the recognition accorded to physics, chemistry, biology, and the rest of the natural or physical sciences. The reasons for this are simple. In the first place, the social sciences do not lend themselves to experimentation; it is not allowable to experiment with men or their institutions as you experiment with chemicals, or with animals, in a laboratory. For this reason there is no such testing-out of results as there is, for instance, of chemical or biological theories. But it is just this testing-out that proves or disproves, in the eyes of both theorists and practical men, the worth of a science. It is no wonder, therefore, that the social sciences are not trusted as are the natural sciences.

Further, the materials worked upon in the social sciences are men and their ways of doing things. But men and societies are complicated things. They are not like chemical elements, always the same, but are variable, changeable, and unstable. Hence the best one can hope for in the social sciences is a high degree of probability. Almost never can precision and exactitude of prediction be attained. There are too many influencing factors in the field. Prediction has to confine itself to tendencies rather than to definite actions. All this makes results less certain, definite, and striking.

And yet there is no doubt in any educated person's mind that behind the institutional adjustments made to life-conditions by mankind lie laws that can be studied out. The life of human societies is not an irregular, disorderly affair, even though it does not go on with the order and precision observable in a bee-hive. The laboratory of the social sciences is really history; it is not so good as a chemical laboratory, for the student of society has to take what experiments the genius presiding over human destiny has seen fit to perform — and these experiments have been loosely done and not very well recorded. Also they have not been done over again in exactly the same way; history, we are told, never repeats itself. For all these reasons the study of society is an extremely difficult and baffling one.

Nevertheless we have come to know something about the nature of human society and the laws that lie behind its adjustments to its life-condition. Human institutions reveal an evolution comparable with that of animals — a connected series of forms evolving out of preceding forms in adjustment to life-conditions. The law of adjustment is present here as elsewhere. And even though we cannot discover, test up, and predict as exactly here as we can in the natural sciences, still it is better to know even somewhat vaguely what laws are at work, and what to expect, than to go it blind. And we can hope, by resolute attention to work and by the exercise of great care, to get more knowledge, and in more exact form, as we go forward, so as ultimately to attain greater precision in our results. The study is exceedingly difficult, and it is as yet very young; there is no reason for despair because results come slowly. The trouble with the social sciences now is that there are many who are so impatient for results that they are not willing to do the necessary arduous work, but fly off to a baseless and sentimental theorizing which, in the eyes of sensible men, makes the social sciences ridiculous.

ART

There is another body of knowledge that mankind has developed which, though not commonly called science, is related to it. It is comprehended under the general term " art." Something has been seen of art — of drawing, painting, music — in the chapter on The Arts of Pleasure. There these arts have been viewed from the side of the one who gets pleasure from their results, that is, from appreciation of them. An appeal is made by them to the eye and the ear; but it must not be thought that, even if appreciation may be spontaneous, the appeal may be devoid of artfulness or the artist innocent of knowledge. Feeling on the part of the artist is the final essential, no doubt, but if he is going to be able to arouse feeling in the observer or listener, he must have hard-won technique and also a body of knowledge that is far from coming of itself or by mere inspiration. Too many would-be poets, painters, and musicians have looked for miracles in this field as naïvely as did the savage in the workaday world. Genius itself is always unaccountable, but a good part of the accomplishment of genius is no mystery; it is the result of laboriously learned technique, capacity for unremitting toil, and knowledge of uninteresting facts, all of which have had to be acquired by even a Goethe or a Beethoven.

Science has to do with adjustment to definite and largely permanent conditions; and adjustments to secure the satisfaction of such universal needs as hunger, sex-love, and fear of the spirits have resulted in real institutions, such as property, marriage, and religion. But art is a means of pleasing taste; and taste is an exceedingly changeable thing. No settled institutions for self-gratification have been developed about an interest that is so variable. It is impossible to say that a thing is beautiful, always has been beautiful, and always will be, as one could say that gravitation drags objects toward the center of the earth, always has done so, and always will. The savage likes a dark skin and a flat nose. He admires fat women. Filed teeth in blue gums, nostrils and lips with plugs in them, and ear-lobes that rest on the shoulders by reason of the weight of the brass rings suspended from them appeal to him as beautiful. How can taste for this sort of thing be reconciled with any asserted absolute and eternal type of beauty? In view of the innumerable and conflicting ideas of what is beautiful in form, sound, color, or motion, one is compelled to conclude that there is no absolute beauty at all.

It might once have been said that nobody's taste could endure the daubs of certain contemporary painters; the squeaks, scrapings, and whacks of certain types of modern music; the Senegambian shuffles and gambols of certain modern dances;

or the " barbaric yawp " of certain formless modern verse. In view of such instances it seems that art must represent adjustment to a variable that is verging in no predictable direction — unless, indeed, we are returning to the cave-man types of art, music, and dancing. Long ago it was said that there was no disputing about tastes. Where it is a question of what men like, or think they like, or can be made to think they ought to like, it is evident that no such definite goal lies at the end of study as in the case of science, the results of which will verify, if correct, in any place and at any time. The science of today gets results in adjustment to life-conditions beside which those of even fifty years ago look very simple and childish; but art can show no such steady improvement. It is not possible to compare Greek literature and art, to their disadvantage, with those of any succeeding age. They are not childish at all. No more are the paintings of several centuries ago crude and juvenile beside those of today.

And yet there are certain ways that have been discovered by which results can be attained that seem better adjusted than others, at least to the cultivated eye and ear. Printers know about how long a line of print ought to be in order to be read without strain. Musicians have learned to produce minor strains or martial airs or dance-music in adjustment to sad or patriotic or playful states of mind. Painters and architects have evolved rules of various sorts to guide them in producing pleasing results. And they all have acquired technique that can be taught. The aspiring musician is put through a rigid discipline in harmony and counterpoint that is strongly reminiscent of mathematics; and the literary man must have learned to wield the instrument of language. It is even possible to know, through an application of physics, that sound-waves of certain lengths will blend to form a concord, while others will not do so, but will make discord. In general the human ear does not favor discord unless it has been trained to like it. In general, too, the ear responds to rhythm. There is a pleasing quality about circles, crosses, and other symmetries of design, though taste is found to favor irregularity also. Form and technique are instruments by which feeling is expressed by the artist and evoked in the observer or hearer; and the former has learned rules about using them which represent adjustments to conditions. Men have certainly learned to get pleasure out of things that were once matters of indifference to them. There is a large body of knowledge about form and technique, and there are laws behind form to which an artist can adjust with the result of pleasing what we generally refer to as a refined taste.

Perhaps the performance of art that enjoys the most permanent and invariable success is " holding a mirror up to nature." To do that there is need enough of art, especially if something more than the mere form is to be reproduced. A photograph is mechanically correct; but the skillful painter makes a more " speaking " likeness because he artfully works in that which the camera misses. He shows more in his mirror because it is a more sensitive and refined reflector; and the additional things are the intangible ones. He suggests what he does not actually portray. What is " true to life " is generally admirable and pleasing, provided the subject selected for portrayal is not in itself unlovely or repulsive; if it is, then there is nothing left to admire except the skill of the performer.

Music is perhaps the most direct path to the emotions, and the reproduction in rhythm and tones of the intangible, subtle, and obscure moods of the composer in a form to evoke similar moods in the listener is one of the greatest conquests won by man in the use of a medium of communication. It is foolish to think of music as portraying definite thoughts or sentiments, and compositions which are merely imitative of sounds in nature are scarcely more uplifting than imitative words like " slam " or " bang " or " buzz." At its best, it appeals to vague and obscure longings that are indescribable in words, and sets its hearers off on trains of reflection or musing that are probably not the same in any two cases. This is why it is futile to try to attach titles to the profoundest music.

Then there is another function of art which is, in a sense, the opposite of holding up the mirror, and that lies in the production of illusion. Where life is dull and commonplace, there is no diversion in a realistic presentation of it; what is wanted is romance, for that transports the one who sees or hears into an enjoyable frame of mind or at least diverts him from pre-occupation with the actualities of which he is tired. Poems and tales represent life as it might be if there were no sickness, old age, poverty, and loss; and the reader forgets the inevitability of these ills and lives for a time, in imagination, in a world free from them. It is a great pleasure to become immersed in such experiences; but, like other stimulants and narcotics, romance is a sort of a habit-forming drug. So, indeed, are most if not all pleasurable activities. Even work, when it has become one's only or dominant pleasure, may run out into dissipation.

There is an immense amount of variability in art — necessarily so, because it is an adjustment to so variable a thing as taste. And yet the art-forms of a period are of a piece with the rest of the social forms, and play their part in reflecting what is called " the spirit of the age." Though they may not be subject to rigorous and decisive selection, as are the forms more vital in the struggle for existence — for, so far as continuing to exist is concerned, it makes little difference what sort of art a people has, as compared with its economic or political organization — yet they come nevertheless under that law of adjustment which we have repeatedly shown to be exemplified in the customs and institutions of society.

Anything that makes life easier and happier is second in importance only to what makes life possible. And there is also in art a certain effect of elevation of spirit. The musician and poet have tapped stores of human energy by war-songs and expressions of patriotism; and art in general is always exercising a stress away from the more sordid interests of life. It has been of immense service in representing, preserving, and transmitting religious ideas, and in inducing and supporting religious frames of mind. It has lent a heightened interest to that which otherwise would have been merely utilitarian. It has made life more interesting. Too much attention should not be given to the fads and fancies of art. It is particularly prone to them, and they are not selected away very promptly, for they do not matter very much in the rough-and-tumble of life. But the general service of the fine arts has been as important to mankind as diversion and pleasure and refinement are important amidst the hard and often sordid work of living.

CHAPTER XIII

EDUCATION

To the youth who is facing the struggle for existence in a savage society the value of what he learns is a matter of daily experience, for it all has an immediate bearing on life and welfare. If he is told to go quietly when hunting, and does not, he is automatically punished by failure to get game. This means that he goes hungry, or is humiliated by his failure, or both; and he will be eager to avoid such a result the next time. In such cases he does not need to be disciplined, because negligence or disobedience will bring its own penalty, and a severe one at that. If he is careless enough perhaps he will be killed, which will remove him from the ranks of the unruly once and for all, and also serve as an object-lesson and an excellent demonstration of the value of teachableness. Primitive education does not get very far from the immediate conditions of life, and so is verified all the time upon those conditions.

Not a few of the foolish educational projects of the time would stand condemned on the face of them if they were to be judged in the light of the principle which even savages unwittingly follow: that education is an adjustment whereby the rising generation become useful to the society in which they are to pass their lives. All studies started by being "practical," and by being recognized as such. The boy of the mediæval period knew why he was studying Latin. That language was in constant use, in the law-courts and elsewhere; most books of the time were written in it; to know it was a mark of culture which secured very practical advantages to the possessor. It opened careers. It is not possible nowadays thus to see, from the beginning of a study, its practical utility to the one who masters it. A good deal of modern education has to be taken on faith or simply because authority commands it; and the result is that there is more resistance on the part of learners and more need of compulsion than there was on the more primitive stage. Penalties for non-performance have to be invented to take the place of those which nature once imposed, for there is no immediate and convincing test any longer at hand.

The natural way to learn things is by imitation; and most of the customary ways of living and acting are appropriated in that natural way. Education is a more artificial process. Certain ways of doing things are selected by some authority with a view of impressing them upon the ignorant. These ways and this knowledge are thought to be particularly important for some purpose, or they would not be picked out for learning from among the innumerable things which are learnable. The purpose is to make the learner more efficient in some way, and what is set before him depends upon the idea of efficiency that is in the mind of the educator. It follows that there are as many notions about what should be learned as there are ideas about efficiency.

But if we go back toward the beginning of things, where there are no professional educators to think out programs, we find that the young are taught what is going to make them useful members of society. No one reflects upon what will and what will not have that effect, for savages cannot think in terms of societies; but the boys are taught what an efficient man should know and the girls are schooled in the duties of the sort of wife who is indispensable on that stage of development. This all works out for the welfare of the society, of course; for any society is better off if its members are proficient in the regular functions that keep life going smoothly. Consequently the boys are early removed from their mothers' influence, and thrown under that of the men; and the girls are left to learn from the women. Home-teaching, which is always, whether it succeeds or fails, the most important and decisive of all, ends early; and the loss is small, for there is none of that sympathy and intimacy of relationship between parents and children, and none of those fine shadings of good breeding to be learned, which make of the modern home a school with possibilities possessed by no other.

It is possible to learn the character of the schooling provided by any educational agency by noting the type and matter of the test required for passing or graduation. The savages subject both sexes, when they come to the age of puberty, to such a test, the general nature of which is an inquiry into whether the boy is ready to enter into the ranks of the men, or warriors, or husbands, and the girl to enter upon the career of a wife. Such ordeals are sometimes called marriage-tests, because marriage is likely to come soon to those who thus qualify for it. Before he is fit to marry, the boy must often submit to severe physical torture to prove his courage; must demonstrate his powers as a hunter, and so as a provider for a family, by tracking and killing game; must take the scalp or bring in the skull of some enemy, to prove his worth in fighting; or must otherwise qualify for the title of man and warrior. The girl must show skill and energy in planting and weeding, preparing skins and making garments, cooking, and other of the accomplishments of an efficient house-wife. This constitutes the general type of primitive education. Of course much of it is learned by unconscious imitation and in play, but there is really some instruction deliberately given.

Among backward peoples there is also a special kind of professional education which selected youths (in rare instances, girls) may acquire; and that is the training in magical matters needful to become a medicine-man. Ordinary people learn from one another, and especially from some particularly skillful person, the best methods of stone-working, metal-working, and the like, and there are traditions and songs that are passed along from one generation to another; but there is no other such " course " as the aspirant to the office of magician must go through, unless it is the training for smithery — and the smith is widely reputed to be a wizard. The fact of it is that the medicine-man and priests form the only class in society which has more knowledge than the common herd — a secret knowledge, or false knowledge, or set of superstitions, which they jealously guard, and out of which, in the end and by endless correction, science is evolved. Thus the germ of knowledge beyond the ordinary is seen, again, to take its start within a body of superstition.

The youth who aims to become a medicine-man or priest is put through fastings and tortures first, to discover whether he is fit. Fitness is proved by the endurance shown and also by the visions and trances that come to a brain disordered by the faintness of hunger and the throes of bodily pain. Then, having passed the ordeal, he is instructed; and he knows from observation and experience the value of th to us, mostly worthless stuff which he is taught. He has seen the honor accorded to the magician and the fear and awe inspired by him; and he has realized the number and size of the fees that can be collected. He does not have to be persuaded of the worth of what he is learning; and he knows that as soon as he graduates, he can apply all he knows to his own exceeding advantage. On the primitive stage, all learning is of direct and immediate utility, with no long periods to be spent in the acquisition of things whose utility does not appear.

And so the novice learns all the hocus-pocus of charms, dances, incantations, magic mixtures and " medicines," and all the rest, with industry and avidity. Some of the knowledge he gets is really worth while, even from our point of view, though he cannot account in any rational way for the results — in the curing of diseases, for instance — which he actually effects. For, as elsewhere mentioned, the " doctors," starting with what we should call a false theory of disease, and exploring about for means of driving out the spirits which they regarded as the troublesome agents, hit upon such effective processes as massage and such real medicines as quinine. These were the few grains of wheat in the bushels of chaff, perhaps, but they were wheat all the same.

For many ages education did not go much beyond what has just been indicated. It was not so long ago that a boy was expected to occupy the same station in life as his father, and was supposed to learn what was necessary, in agriculture, smithery, carpentry, or other occupation or trade, from him. Or he might be apprenticed to some craftsman and gradually accumulate enough knowledge and skill to set up for himself. Girls still learned the lessons of the house-wife in the home, and what education there was was almost wholly practical. It was still the priestly class that monopolized general knowledge, starting with reading and writing.

Only in modern times and among the most civilized nations has it come to be believed that education ought, for the welfare of society, to be assured to everyone, both male and female. And what the masses of the people have been taught in public schools has remained, for the most part and until the modern invasion of those schools by fads and theories, almost wholly the so-called elements, or " three R's " — reading, writing, and arithmetic — together with some geography and history. Any citizen is the better, it is thought, for not being illiterate. And in a country like this the public school has discharged an added function, and one most important for the nation's well-being, namely, that of an agency for removing differences in language and customs. In this country, with its large yearly influx of foreigners, such molding of the young to the national type is called " Americanization "; and it has been an adjustment productive of mutual understanding and sympathy, and almost indispensable to national unity.

With the development of science and art there has been more knowledge to offer to those who could take advantage of it; but the education thus available has naturally demanded more time, and its application to the practical affairs of life has become less immediately obvious. The ultimate object of higher studies, so-called, has not been visible from the outset; they could not be tested out directly, like the precepts for hunting or metal-working, and the student has not had that same incentive to learn that spurred the youth who could see from the start the goal at which he was to arrive and the practical advantages of attaining it. Many young men and women go on with high school and college studies because it is the thing to do, or for other reasons that have nothing to do with the high valuation of studies for themselves and for what they may bring. Ignorant people are always resisting the laws which compel even a certain minimum of schooling beyond the most elementary, wishing their children to cut short further preparation for living and get to work at once. Neither class values education for what it is worth.

It is certain that higher education has become a sort of mania in some countries, notably our own. The tremendous expense of providing it for ever larger numbers is ignored. It is assumed that every one should have it, and many who would be useful citizens in an humbler capacity are being urged or forced through a course of higher education for which they are quite unfitted. This results in the lowering of the standards of higher education and the undue heightening of the expectations of persons of lower capacity. If every one has the *chance* at a higher education, then, if one is man enough to take it without much urging or coercing or help, it will be a good thing both for him and for the community. But it is irrational to consider it a right assured to everybody, irrespective of his fitness and his own exertions. It is a privilege, rather, to be reserved for those who prove themselves. As such it would not be cheapened and lowered in standard by being overrun and swamped under the weight of unselected numbers.

Before the development of science, higher education was

is in the way of acquiring a feeling for the welfare of his community or nation which will prevent him from becoming utterly one-sided, short-sighted, and selfish.

By study also the student can become not only broad-minded, but mentally disciplined. His mind ceases to be lawlessly inclined, like that of a child or an ignoramus. "No person can be called educated who will not do effectively something that he does not wish to do at the time when it ought to be done." Also he knows what he can do with his mind and has learned to use it on all sorts of problems. He does not recoil in despair before puzzling situations, for he knows how to go at them, because he has seen how men have met difficulties before, and he has acquired the tested methods for dealing with such difficulties. If he realizes that new puzzles are nothing but new complications of old ones, and if he knows how the old ones were surmounted, he cannot be utterly befogged in dealing with the new ones. He need not, at least, fall into terror and despair but can retain presence of mind, at any rate, and a conviction that a solution is possible. In some cases he can know that certain proposed solutions are probably impossible, for they have been tried, perhaps over and over again, as the inflation of currency has been tried, and have never worked out.

Just as a man may remember and profit by his past experience, so may he assist society to profit by its past errors and successes, if he knows about them and understands how to apply his knowledge to cases that arise. There can never be so very many persons who have had the opportunity of acquiring such fitness to assist in directing the destinies of their communities or nations, and still fewer who have the capacity to acquire that fitness, even when they see the opportunity and seek to grasp it; but it is evident that those few are a great asset to any society. So are those who are educated enough to understand and support these natural leaders, even if they cannot rise to leadership themselves. Great men cannot succeed

without support; and one of the basic services of education is
to provide an understanding clientage for the great men. It is
evident that education is for a society an adjustment of the
most permanent and fundamental nature, enabling it to meet
its life-conditions with a success it could not hope for in the
absence of citizens of understanding and vision, and with disciplined minds, who can appreciate the emotions and interests
of the masses of men and guide them to expedient expression.

To get an asset of this kind, education must aim at it. It
must seek to produce, not narrow specialists, but all-round
minds. There are specialists who attain notable successes in
some restricted fields, but who are wholly uneducated in the
sense of which we are speaking — the only true sense. No one
would think of intrusting them with positions of power, or
even of wasting time in listening to their opinions on matters
of broad social policy. They are hopelessly lopsided because
their training has been so specialized. Such are scientists who
have no knowledge of the humanities, or humanists who are in
the dark as to nature and methods of science. What society
needs is a well-balanced educational product — one who can
appreciate the nature and aims of all branches of knowledge,
though he is not able, of course, to follow each specialist into
the technical details of his specialty. It was once said of the
cultured man that nothing human is foreign to him; and if a
man is serious enough in his studies, he presently finds out
that all knowledge is one — not separated off into little, un-
connected, narrow canals, but a single, broad stream of inter-
mixing currents. When he discovers this, then he has acquired
an insight into life and life-conditions that makes him exceedingly valuable to his time.

After getting his general bearings in the world of knowledge,
one is ready to specialize in some line; and his choice will
be an intelligent one, for now he sees the various possibilities
in their relation to one another. And he is ready to go into the
practice of some specialty, whether it is business, trade, or pro-

fession, and not lose himself in it; for when he has once seen the woods as a whole, he will have a sort of reconnaissance-map, so that he will not wander aimlessly from tree to tree.

It was said several pages back that the result of what primitive education there was consisted in training a boy or girl to take his place in the tribe or society, as an efficient member of it. That is what education still does, if it is to promote social welfare. The older must soon die, and the young must take their places and carry on. To do that they must learn what the older have succeeded in living by. Once there was not much to learn, and what there was to learn was very simple and obviously useful; now there is a great deal, and much of it is not so simple and obvious in its application. Formerly nearly every one could learn all there was to know; now there are few who can even appreciate what there is to know, much less learn it all. The most that can be hoped for now is to have every one who is not mentally defective learn the simplest and most elementary things, and to give each the chance to advance beyond the elements as far as his ability and energy can carry him.